Kids
SUMMER
ACADEMY
ARGOPREP

7 DAYS A WEEK
12 WEEKS

Mathematics
English
Science
Reading
Writing

Fitness
Yoga
Experiments
Mazes
Puzzles

GRADE 3-4

ArgoPrep is one of the leading providers of supplemental educational products and services. We offer affordable and effective test prep solutions to educators, parents and students. Learning should be fun and easy! For that reason, most of our workbooks come with detailed video answer explanations taught by one of our fabulous instructors.

Our goal is to make your life easier, so let us know how we can help you by e-mailing us at:
info@argoprep.com.

TABLE OF CONTENTS

TABLE OF CONTENTS

TABLE OF CONTENTS

TABLE OF CONTENTS

HOW TO USE THE BOOK

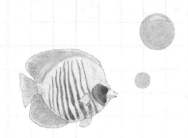

Welcome to **Kids Summer Academy** by ArgoPrep.

This workbook is designed to prepare students over the summer to get ready for **Grade 4**. The curriculum has been divided into **twelve weeks** so students can complete this entire workbook over the summer.

Our workbook has been carefully designed and **crafted by licensed teachers** to give students an incredible learning experience.

Students start off the week with English activities followed by Math practice. Throughout the week, students have several fitness activities to complete. Making sure students stay active is just as important as practicing mathematics.

We introduce yoga and other basic fitness activities that any student can complete. Each week includes a science experiment which sparks creativity and allows students to visually understand the concepts. On the last day of each week, students will work on a fun puzzle.

HOW TO WATCH VIDEO EXPLANATIONS
IT IS ABSOLUTELY FREE

Step 1 - Visit our website at: www.argoprep.com/books

Step 2 - Click on the JOIN FOR FREE button located on the top right corner.

Step 3 - Choose the grade level workbook you have.

Step 4 - Sign up as a Learner, Parent or a Teacher.

Step 5 - Register using your email or social networks.

Step 6 - From your dashboard cick on FREE WORKBOOKS EXPLANATION on the left and choose the workbook you have.

You now have life time access to the video explanations for your workbook!

WHAT TO READ OVER THE SUMMER

One of the best ways to increase your reading comprehension level is to read a book for at least **20** minutes a day. We strongly encourage students to read several books throughout the summer. Below you will find a recommended summer reading list that we have compiled for students entering into Grade 4 or simply visit us at: www.argobrothers.com/**summerlist**

Author: Traci Sorell
Title: We Are Grateful

Author: Judy Blume
Title: Tales of a Fourth Grade Nothing

Author: Rob Laidlaw
Title: Bat Citizens: Defending the Ninjas of the Night

Author: Rebecca Stead
Title: When you Reach Me

Author: Betsy Bird
Title: Funny Girl: Funniest. Stories. Ever.

Author: Lynne Reid Banks
Title: The Indian in the Cupboard

Author: Judy Blume
Title: Blubber

Author: Lois Lowry
Title: Number the Stars

Author: Christopher Paul Curtis
Title: Bud, Not Buddy

Author: Jen Bryant
Title: Six Dots: A Story of Young Louis Braille

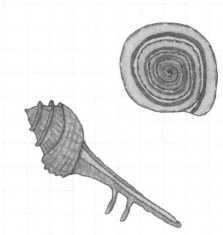

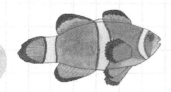

OTHER BOOKS BY ARGOPREP

Here are some other test prep workbooks by ArgoPrep you may be interested in. All of our workbooks come equipped with detailed video explanations to make your learning experience a breeze! Visit us at www.argoprep.com

COMMON CORE SERIES

  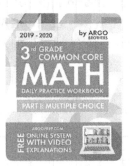 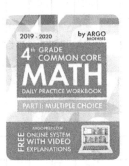

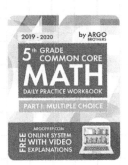   

SPECIALIZED HIGH SCHOOL ADMISSIONS TEST

HIGHER LEVEL EXAMS

INTRODUCING MATH!

Introducing Math! by ArgoPrep is an award-winning series created by certified teachers to provide students with high-quality practice problems. Our workbooks include topic overviews with instruction, practice questions, answer explanations along with digital access to video explanations. Practice in confidence - with ArgoPrep!

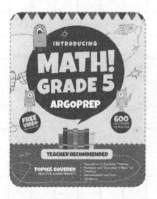  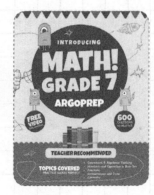 

YOGA MINDFULNESS

If you are looking for a fun way to engage with your children while helping them build a mindful, engaged and healthy lifestyle, Frogyogi's Yoga Stories for Kids and Parents is the perfect book for you and your family!

KIDS SUMMER ACADEMY SERIES

ArgoPrep's **Kids Summer Academy** series helps prevent summer learning loss and gets students ready for their new school year by reinforcing core foundations in math, english and science. Our workbooks also introduce new concepts so students can get a head start and be on top of their game for the new school year!

Welcome! Meet the ArgoPrep heroes.

Are you ready to go on an incredible adventure and complete your journey with them to become a **SUPER** student?

WATER FIRE

MYSTICAL NINJA

FIRESTORM WARRIOR

GREEN POISON

RAPID NINJA

CAPTAIN ARGO

THUNDER WARRIOR

ADRASTOS THE SUPER WARRIOR

Give your character a name

_____

Write down the special ability or powers your character has and how you will help your community with the powers.

_____

_____

Great! You are all set. To become an incredible hero, we need to strengthen our skills in **english**, **math** and **science**. Let's get started.

Are you ready to start your journey? Let's dive right into week I.

WEEK I

Did you know our oceans cover more than 70 percent of the Earth's surface?

It's also estimated that roughly 70% of the oxygen we breathe is produced by the ocean from marine plants. How cool is that!

ARGOPREP

As your vocabulary grows, it's important to understand how to express ideas using a variety of different words. One way writers do this, is by adding certain beginnings or endings to words that change or deepen their meaning. It's important that you know how to attach prefixes and suffixes to words for your own writing, but it's equally important to be able to identify and define them as you read.

 Key Terms

Root Word: a basic word that you would use in a sentence

Prefix: letters added <u>before</u> the beginning of a root word to change or add to the meaning

For Example...

Root Word: Happy (joyful or content)
Prefix: Un- (meaning "not")
New Word: Unhappy (meaning "<u>not</u> joyful or content")

In a sentence: My sister was <u>unhappy</u> that the tooth fairy only left her a nickel.

Root Word: Sentence (a complete thought expressed in words)
Prefix: Mid (meaning "in the middle of")
New Word: Mid-sentence (meaning "in the middle of a sentence")

In a sentence: I get frustrated when people interrupt me <u>mid-sentence.</u>

Common Prefixes

Prefix	Definition	Example
Anti-	Fighting against	Antibacterial (fighting against bacteria) Antiaging (fighting the aging process)
Auto-	To one's self	Autobiography (a book about yourself) Automatic (working by itself)
De-	To cancel out, reverse, or remove	Debug (to remove bugs or glitches from software) Destruct (to reverse the process of something being constructed)

Prefix	Definition	Example
Mid-	In the middle of	Mid-year (in the middle of the year) Midfield (in the middle of the field)
Mis-	Done badly or incorrectly	Mislead (to lead people in the wrong direction) Miscalculate (to do math wrong)
Pre-	Before	Prewar (before the war) Prejudge (to judge before having the facts)
Post-	After	Postwar (after the war) Postseason (the part of the sports schedule after the main season)
Re-	Again	Rediscover (to find something again) Redo (to do again or do over)
Trans-	Across or Change	Transatlantic (across the Atlantic Ocean) Transform (changing something's form or appearance)
Un-	Not	Unhappy (not happy) Undo (reverse something that was done)

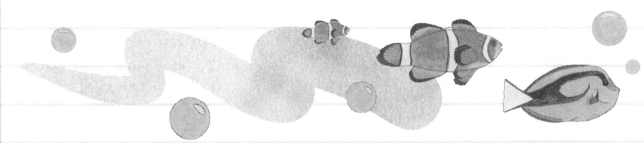

The Hare With Many Friends
By Aesop

A Hare was very popular with the other beasts who all claimed to be her friends. But one day she heard the hounds approaching and hoped to escape them by the aid of her many Friends. So, she went to the horse, and asked him to carry her away from the hounds on his back. But he declined, stating that he had important work to do for his master. "I feel sure," he said, "that all your other friends will come to her assistance."

She then applied to the bull, and hoped that he would repel the hounds with his horns. The bull replied: "I am very sorry, but I have an appointment with a lady; but I feel sure that our friend the goat will do what you want."

The goat, however, feared that his back might do her some harm if he took her upon it. The ram, he felt sure, was the proper friend to apply to. So she went to the ram and told him the case. The ram replied: "Another time, my dear friend. I do not like to interfere on the present occasion, as hounds have been known to eat sheep as well as hares."

The Hare then applied, as a last hope, to the calf, who regretted that he was unable to help her, as he did not like to take the responsibility upon himself, as so many older persons than himself had declined the task. By this time the hounds were quite near, and the Hare took to her heels and luckily escaped.

He that has many friends, has no friends.

1. Why is the Hare seeking help from her friends?

2. Why is the phrase "who all claimed to be" in the first sentence important to the rest of the story?

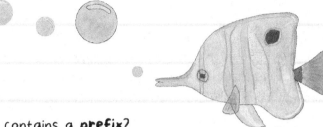
3. Which animal tries to convince the Hare that it will actually hurt her worse if it tries to help her?

   A. The horse
   B. The bull
   C. The goat
   D. The calf

4. Which of these phrases from the passage contains a **prefix**?

   A. The horse was sure "all your other friends will come"
   B. The bull said he "had an appointment with a lady"
   C. The ram is concerned that "hounds have been known to eat sheep as well as hares"
   D. The calf said "he was unable to help her"

5. How does the Hare's story connect to the author's point that, "He that has many friends, has no friends"?

Identifying and Defining Words with Prefixes

⭐ **Directions:**

Circle the word in each sentence that uses a prefix. Then, on the line below, write a short definition for that word based on your understanding of the prefix.

1. Saturday's soccer game was very frustrating because the referees appeared to be completely untrained.

2. The printer got completely jammed up because I misaligned the paper when I filled it.

3. Mr. Francis allows students to retake his quizzes if they score below a **75%**.

4. The autocorrect function on cell phones and word processing programs cannot always be trusted.

5. If a web page is not loading correctly, it can be useful to hit the refresh button and allow the process to start over.

FITNESS

Please be aware of your environment and be safe at all times. If you cannot do an exercise, just try your best.

2 - Lunges: 2 times to each leg.
Note: Use your body weight or books as weight to do leg lunges.

1 - Abs: 3 times   Repeat these **exercises 3 ROUNDS**

4 - Run: 50m
Note: Run 25 meters to one side and 25 meters back to the starting position.

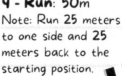

3 - Plank: 6 sec.

Saving the Birds
By James Baldwin

One day in spring four men were riding on horseback along a country road. These men were lawyers, and they were going to the next town to attend court. There had been a rain, and the ground was very soft. Water was dripping from the trees, and the grass was wet. The four lawyers rode along, one behind another; for the pathway was narrow, and the mud on each side of it was deep. They rode slowly, and talked and laughed and were very jolly.

As they were passing through a grove of small trees, they heard a great fluttering over their heads and a feeble chirping in the grass by the roadside.

"Stith! stith! stith!" came from the leafy branches above them.

"Cheep! cheep! cheep!" came from the wet grass.

"What is the matter here?" asked the first lawyer, whose name was Speed. "Oh, it's only some old robins!" said the second lawyer, whose name was Hardin. "The storm has blown two of the little ones out of the nest. They are too young to fly, and the mother bird is making a great fuss about it."

"What a pity! They'll die down there in the grass," said the third lawyer, whose name I forget.

"Oh, well! They're nothing but birds," said Mr. Hardin. "Why should we bother?"

"Yes, why should we?" said Mr. Speed.

The three men, as they passed, looked down and saw the little birds fluttering in the cold, wet grass. They saw the mother robin flying about, and crying to her mate.

Then they rode on, talking and laughing as before. In a few minutes they had forgotten about the birds.

But the fourth lawyer, whose name was Abraham Lincoln, stopped. He got down from his horse and very gently took the little ones up in his big warm hands.

They did not seem frightened, but chirped softly, as if they knew they were safe.

"Never mind, my little fellows," said Mr. Lincoln "I will put you in your own cozy little bed."

Then he looked up to find the nest from which they had fallen. It was high, much higher than he could reach.

But Mr. Lincoln could climb. He had climbed many a tree when he was a boy. He put the birds softly, one by one, into their warm little home. Two other baby birds were there, that had not fallen out. All cuddled down together and were very happy.

Soon the three lawyers who had ridden ahead stopped at a spring to give their horses water.

"Where is Lincoln?" asked one.

All were surprised to find that he was not with them.

"Do you remember those birds?" said Mr. Speed. "Very likely he has stopped to take care of them."

In a few minutes Mr. Lincoln joined them. His shoes were covered with mud; he had torn his coat on the thorny tree.

"Hello, Abraham!" said Mr. Hardin. "Where have you been?"

"I stopped a minute to give those birds to their mother," he answered.

"Well, we always thought you were a hero," said Mr. Speed. "Now we know it."

Then all three of them laughed heartily. They thought it so foolish that a strong man should take so much trouble just for some worthless young birds.

"Gentlemen," said Mr. Lincoln, "I could not have slept to-night, if I had left those helpless little robins to perish in the wet grass."

Abraham Lincoln afterwards became very famous as a lawyer and statesman. He was elected president. Next to Washington he was the greatest American.

1. How is Abraham Lincoln different from the other characters in the passage?

2. Which of these words with a prefix describes the three other lawyers traveling with Lincoln?

   A. Misunderstanding
   B. Unhelpful
   C. Anti-bird
   D. Post-travels

3. Which event in the story shows that Abraham Lincoln was willing to help others, even when it was inconvenient for him?

4. How do the other lawyers feel about Abraham Lincoln?

5. How do you know that the author of the passage admired Abraham Lincoln a great deal?

⭐ **Directions:**

Fill in the blank by adding one of the <u>Common Prefixes</u> to the word in parentheses at the end of the sentence. Be sure to reread the sentence with your new word in place to make sure it makes sense!

1. Maria's nail polish cracked while she was working in the science lab, so she had to _____ it. (APPLY)

2. Most commercial airlines use an _____ system, which means the cockpit crew can focus most of their time planning routes and communicating with air traffic control instead of flying the plane. (PILOT)

3. Even though Mark is a nice guy, I find him _____ because he can't keep a secret. (TRUSTWORTHY)

4. Before computers and copy machines, people had to _____ books by hand, which meant copying every last word onto new pieces of paper. (SCRIBE)

5. Many people use _____ techniques to help them relax and forget about their troubles. (STRESS)

FITNESS

Please be aware of your environment and be safe at all times. If you cannot do an exercise, just try your best.

Repeat these **exercises 3 ROUNDS**

2 - Side Bending: 5 times to each side. Note: try to touch your feet.

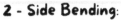

1 - Squats: 5 times. Note: imagine you are trying to sit on a chair.

3 - Tree Pose: Stay as long as possible. Note: do the same with the other leg.

Addition Practice Questions

1. What is the sum of **246** and **352**?

    A. 568
    B. 598
    C. 618
    D. 628

2. Which addition sentence equals to 1,025?

    A. 457 + 568
    B. 563 + 492
    C. 371 + 634
    D. 496 + 589

3. What is **564** added to **126**?

    Answer _____

4. What is **289 + 325**?

    Answer _____

5. What is the sum of **45, 28** and **31**?

    A. 98
    B. 104
    C. 112
    D. 114

6. What is the missing number in this equation?

    $$78 + \_\_\_\_\_ = 891$$

    A. 793
    B. 803
    C. 813
    D. 823

7. What is the sum of **289, 103** and **461**?

    Answer _____

8. What is the sum of **765** and **341**?

    Answer _____

9. Which equation is true?

    A. 347 + 168 = 505
    B. 684 + 127 = 821
    C. 373 + 548 = 911
    D. 467 + 473 = 940

10. Which equation is FALSE?

    A. 652 + 387 = 1,039
    B. 448 + 551 = 1,009
    C. 574 + 458 = 1,032
    D. 345 + 695 = 1,040

Subtraction Practice Questions

1. What is the difference between **857** and **324**?

    A. 543
    B. 533
    C. 532
    D. 523

2. What is **568** subtracted from **1,120**?

    Answer _____

3. What is the missing number in this equation?

    $$787 - _____ = 304$$

    Answer _____

4. Choose the expression that is true.

    A. 1,368 - 124 = 1,244
    B. 1,257 - 1,136 = 125
    C. 786 - 541 = 255
    D. 689 - 352 = 347

5. What is **975 - 346 - 154**?

    Answer _____

6. Choose the option that has a value less than the difference between **637** and **358**.

   A. 289
   B. 269
   C. 299
   D. 309

7. Which expression is FALSE?

   A. 562 - 397 = 165
   B. 473 - 189 = 284
   C. 735 - 697 = 48
   D. 464 - 277 = 187

8. Which expression is true?

   A. 638 - 285 = 363
   B. 864 - 783 = 81
   C. 591 - 386 = 215
   D. 748 - 359 = 379

9. What is 834 - 562?

   Answer _____

10. What is 347 subtracted from 1,007?

    Answer _____

FITNESS

Repeat these **exercises 3 ROUNDS**

Please be aware of your environment and be safe at all times. If you cannot do an exercise, just try your best.

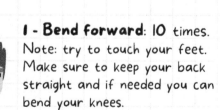

1 - Bend forward: 10 times. Note: try to touch your feet. Make sure to keep your back straight and if needed you can bend your knees.

2 - Lunges: 3 times to each leg. Note: Use your body weight or books as weight to do leg lunges.

3 - Plank: 6 sec.

4 - Abs: 10 times

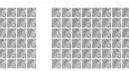
Multiplication Practice Questions

1. What is 8 × 30?

   A. 240
   B. 830
   C. 24
   D. 83

2. Choose a pair of numbers that results in a product of **560**?

   A. 7 and 8
   B. 70 and 80
   C. 70 and 8
   D. 700 and 800

3. Which expression best represents the picture below?

   A. 9 + 5
   B. 9 + 9 + 9 + 9 + 9
   C. 5 + 5 + 5 + 5 + 5 + 5 + 5 + 5 + 5
   D. 9 + 5 + 5 + 5 + 5

4. Which picture represents 6 × 8?

   1   2   3   4

   A. 1
   B. 2
   C. 3
   D. 4

5. Which expression is true?

   A. 7 + 7 + 7 + 7 = 7 + 4
   B. 8 + 8 + 8 + 4 = 8 × 4
   C. 20 + 20 + 20 = 20 × 3
   D. 5 + 5 + 5 + 40 = 5 × 40

6. Write a multiplication expression which is represented by the model below?

   Answer _____

7. What is the missing number in this equation?

   $$80 \times \underline{} = 320$$

   Answer _____

8. Which expression is the same as (30 × 4) + (6 × 4)?

   A. 30 + 6 × 4
   B. 36 × 4
   C. 30 × 4 + 6
   D. 30 × (4 + 6)

9. What is 4 × 26?

   Answer _____

10. Find 70 × 9.

    Answer _____

Division Practice Questions

1. Which expression best represents the picture below?

   A. 5 ÷ 3
   B. 15 ÷ 5
   C. 5 ÷ 15
   D. 3 ÷ 5

FITNESS

Repeat these **exercises 3 ROUNDS**

Please be aware of your environment and be safe at all times. If you cannot do an exercise, just try your best.

1 - High Plank: 6 sec.

2 - Chair: 10 sec.
Note: sit on an imaginary chair, keep your back straight.

3 - Waist Hooping: 10 times. Note: if you do not have a hoop, pretend you have an imaginary hoop and rotate your hips 10 times.

4 - Abs: 10 times

Division Practice Questions

1. Which equation could be represented by the picture below?

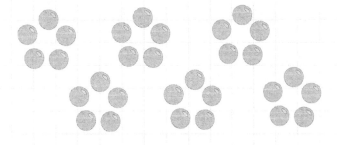

   A. 30 ÷ 5 = 5
   B. 5 ÷ 30 = 6
   C. 30 ÷ 6 = 5
   D. 30 ÷ 6 = 6

2. What is 480 ÷ 6?

   Answer _____

3. What is the quotient when 99 is divided by 9?

   Answer _____

4. Choose the number sentence below that has a quotient of 60.

   A. 540 ÷ 9
   B. 640 ÷ 8
   C. 320 ÷ 4
   D. 480 ÷ 6

5. Which number sentence below is FALSE?

   A. 240 ÷ 8 = 30
   B. 84 ÷ 4 = 80 ÷ 4 + 4 ÷ 4
   C. 56 ÷ 8 = 56 ÷ 7
   D. 45 ÷ 5 = (40 + 5) ÷ 5

6. Find the divider of 810 to get 90.

   Answer _____

7. What is the missing number in the equation 48 ÷ _____ = 12?

   Answer _____

8. What is the missing number in the equation ___ ÷ 24 = 5?

   Answer _____

9. How many times is the number 270 greater than the number 3?

   Answer _____

Word problems: Mix of add/subtract/multiply/divide

1. Charlie has 3 books with 285 pages in each book. How many pages are there in total for the three books?

   A. 825
   B. 855
   C. 865
   D. 885

2. Mr. Anderson has 8 students and he gave each of them 4 word problems. Which expression represents how to find the number of word problems he gave out altogether?

   A. 4 + 8
   B. 8 + 8 + 8
   C. 4 + 4 + 4 + 4 + 4 + 4 + 4 + 4
   D. 4 + 4 + 4 + 4 + 4 + 4

3. Mark has 8 brownies and 9 cakes in each box. If he has 7 boxes, how many brownies and cakes does he have altogether?

   A. 119
   B. 107
   C. 131
   D. 98

4. Cara bought **320** cookies. She had to put them into **8** boxes. How many cookies did Cara put into each box?

   A. 44
   B. 30
   C. 40
   D. 36

5. Grace scored **96** points, which was **3** times more than Carter. How many points did Carter score?

   A. 31
   B. 32
   C. 33
   D. 34

6. Wyatt collected **23** fewer toy cars than Michael. If Michael collected **75** toy cars, how many toy cars did Wyatt collect?

   Answer _____

7. Scarlett wants to buy a **$340** phone. She has saved **$100** and thinks she can save **$60** per month. How many months will it take her to save enough money to buy the phone?

   Answer _____

8. If Mr. Miller split **72** pencils among **12** students, how many pencils did each student receive?

   Answer _____

9. There are **135** potato plants and **148** cucumber plants. How many plants are there in all?

   Answer _____

10. Hans had **1,126** yellow stars. If he gave **214** to his sister, how many stars did Hans have left?

    Answer _____

YOGA

Please be aware of your environment and be safe at all times. If you cannot do an exercise, just try your best.

1 - Down Dog: 10 sec.

4 - Child Pose: 20 sec.

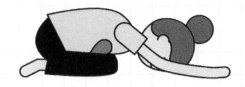

2 - Bend Down: 10 sec.

5 - Shavasana: as long as you can. Note: think of happy moments and relax your mind.

3 - Chair: 10 sec.

Comparing Mass by Making a Balance

All objects have **mass**. Mass is a measurement of **how much** material something is made out of. Mass is different than weight because mass is constant, while weight is partially determined by the force of gravity (for example, your weight would be different on the Moon than it is on Earth because of the differences in gravity, but your mass would be the same!)

A **balance** is a device that scientists use to measure or compare masses. Today, we'll be making a balance that you can use to compare the masses of different household objects.

Materials:

- Plastic Coat Hanger
- Yarn, string, or twine (about 4-5 feet total)
- A tape measure or ruler
- Scissors
- Hole Punch (optional)
- Assorted small household objects (must fit into one of the cups!)

Procedure:

1. Using the hole punch (or scissors, if you don't have one), make two holes just below the rim and directly across from each other in each of the cups, so that the cups can be hung by the string.

2. Using your tape measure or ruler and scissors, cut your length of yarn, string, or twine exactly in half

3. Feed the lengths of string or yarn through the holes you just created in the cup, so that, when you hold the loose ends of the string, the cup is hanging downward with the opening facing up.

4. Tie the loose ends of the lengths of string to the bottom corners of the hanger. One cup should be hanging from the bottom-left corner of the hanger, while the other should be hanging from the bottom-right corner. Make sure the knots are tied so that the two cups are hanging down at the same length. This is important to make sure your balance works accurately!

5. Hook the top of the hanger onto a safe place where both cups can dangle downward.

6. Choose two of the small household objects you gathered and place each of them in one of the cups. One of the cups should hang down lower than the other. This means that the object in that cup has a greater mass!

7. Using your balance and some note paper, compare all the objects you gathered to one another and rank them from highest mass to lowest mass

8. When you're done with this activity, be sure to save your balance because we'll be using it in future experiments as well.

Follow-Up Questions:

1. Why do you think it was important that the lengths of string or yarn were the same?

2. What was the most massive object you put in your balance?

YOGA

Please be aware of your environment and be safe at all times. If you cannot do an exercise, just try your best.

1 - Tree Pose: Stay as long as possible. Note: do on one leg then on another.

2 - Down Dog: 10 sec.

3 - Stretching: Stay as long as possible. Note: do on one leg then on another.

4 - Lower Plank: 6 sec. Note: Keep your back straight and body tight.

5 - Book Pose: 6 sec. Note: Keep your core tight. Legs should be across from your eyes.

6 - Shavasana: 5 min. Note: this pose is very important and provides you with long term benefits. Try not to skip this. Close your eyes and imagine who you want to be and what your goals are! Always think happy thoughts.

31

Task: Help find the way home for these lost tourists. Color in the path they need to take.

Oh yeah!
Looks like you are getting the hang of this. Excited for week 2? I know I sure am!

WEEK 2

Did you know humans have only explored about 5% of the ocean?

There are so many things we do not yet know about our oceans. As we continue to research and improve our technology, we will learn more fascinating facts about our oceans.

ARGOPREP

Key Terms

Root Word: a basic word that you would use in a sentence

Prefix: letters added before the beginning of a root word to change or add to the meaning

Suffix: letters added after the end of a root word to change or add to the meaning

 For Example...

Root Word: Teach (to communicate information or skills to)

Suffix: -able (meaning "capable of being")

New Word: Teachable (meaning "capable of being taught")

In a sentence: I don't know a lot about suffixes yet, but I am very teachable.

Common Suffixes

Suffix	Definition	Example
-able/-ible	Able to do something	Drinkable (able to be drink safely) Flexible (able to flex or bend)
-dom	A situation built around a single idea	Kingdom (a situation in which a king is in charge) Boredom (a situation in which being bored is the main feeling)
-ee	Someone receiving something	Employee (someone receiving employment) Trainee (someone receiving training)
-er/-or	Someone who does something	Swimmer (someone who swims) Creator (someone who creates things)
-ful	Being filled with a certain characteristic	Helpful (filled with the desire to help others) Beautiful (filled with beauty)

Suffix	Definition	Example
-ing	Turns a standard verb into a verbal adjective to describe the present action of the noun	Swimming (the thing you do with your arms and legs in water) Eating (the thing you do at meal time)
-ism	A philosophy or belief system	Traditionalism (the philosophy that old traditions are the best) Buddhism (belief in the philosophy of Buddha)
-ist	A follower of a philosophy or belief system	Traditionalist (someone who believes that old traditions are the best) Buddhist (someone who believes in the philosophy of Buddha)
-less	Without	Homeless (without a home) Friendless (without a friend)
-ness	Turns a descriptive word (adjective) into a thing (noun)	Softness (the feeling that soft things have) Happiness (the feeling of being joyful or content)

The Town Mouse and The Country Mouse
By Aesop

There were once two mice: one who lived in a town, and one who lived out in the country. They were close friends from when they were young, but they led very different lives as adult mice because of their different situations. One year, the Country Mouse invited the Town Mouse to come visit him for a week to catch up and learn more about the freedom of country life.

The Country Mouse showed the Town Mouse how to eat roots and cornstalks that were left in the field, but the Town Mouse didn't enjoy the experience at all. "Out here in the country, you live like an ant!" he told his friend. "It's so hard for you to find food, and then the food you find is plain and dusty. In the town, there's tons of delicious food, and the people make it easy to get to."

The Country Mouse couldn't deny that the town seemed much more convenient, so he followed the Town Mouse back to his home. The Town Mouse showed him how to move from one kitchen to the next through the walls of an apartment building, collecting vegetables, beans, bread, and even honey. The Country Mouse was extremely impressed with how easy it had been to find food and thought that maybe he should move to the town as well.

Once the two mice had assembled a feast, they sat down in one of the kitchens to eat it. However, just as they were about to take a bite, a human opened the front door of the apartment, which scared them so bad they had to run back into the walls. After a few minutes of waiting for the person to pass, the two mice returned the kitchen.

Just as they were about to eat again, the human walked into the kitchen to grab a teacup and screamed at the sight of the two mice. Terrified, the Town Mouse and Country Mouse both retreated into the walls.

"I'm going back home," the hungry Country Mouse told his friend with a frown. "I agree that the food here is outstanding, but is far too dangerous to appreciate!"

1. According to the Town Mouse, why is life in town better than life in the country?

~~~~~~

~~~~~~

2. How does the Country Mouse's experience of the town differ from that of the Town Mouse?

3. Which of these words from the first paragraph uses a suffix to add meaning?

A. Mice
B. Town
C. Lives
D. Freedom

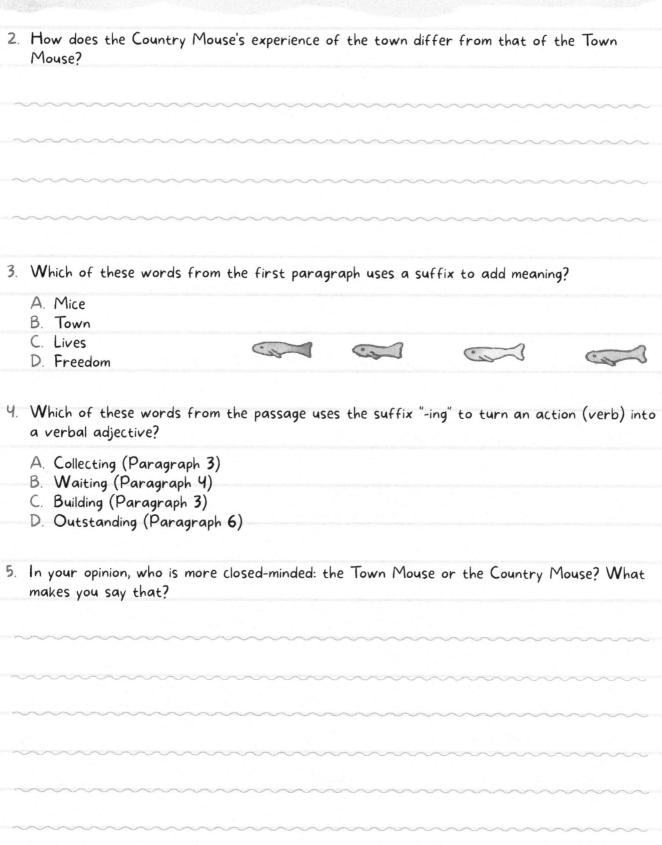

4. Which of these words from the passage uses the suffix "-ing" to turn an action (verb) into a verbal adjective?

A. Collecting (Paragraph 3)
B. Waiting (Paragraph 4)
C. Building (Paragraph 3)
D. Outstanding (Paragraph 6)

5. In your opinion, who is more closed-minded: the Town Mouse or the Country Mouse? What makes you say that?

Identifying and Defining Words with Suffixes

⭐ **Directions:**

Circle the word in each sentence that uses a suffix. Then, on the line below, write a short definition for that word based on your understanding of the suffix.

1. I always try to be cheerful in the morning, but it can be tough!

2. I missed my bus because I was just staring off into space, totally thoughtless.

3. My Aunt Rachel was a great rugby player when she was in college.

4. Some mushrooms are edible, but many of them can make you sick.

5. My brother loves rocking out to music with his headphones on.

 FITNESS

Please be aware of your environment and be safe at all times. If you cannot do an exercise, just try your best.

Repeat these **exercises 3 ROUNDS**

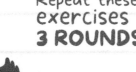

1 - Abs: 3 times

2 - Lunges: 2 times to each leg.
Note: Use your body weight or books as weight to do leg lunges.

4 - Run: 50m
Note: Run 25 meters to one side and 25 meters back to the starting position.

3 - Plank: 6 sec.

The Whistle
By James Baldwin

Two hundred years ago there lived in Boston a little boy whose name was Benjamin Franklin.

On the day that he was seven years old, his mother gave him a few pennies.

He looked at the bright, yellow pieces and said, "What shall I do with these coppers, mother?"

It was the first money that he had ever had.

"You may buy something, if you wish," said his mother.

"And then will you give me more?" he asked.

His mother shook her head and said: "No, Benjamin. I cannot give you any more. So you must be careful not to spend these foolishly."

The little fellow ran into the street. He heard the pennies jingle in his pocket. How rich he was!

Boston is now a great city, but at that time it was only a little town.

There were not many stores.

As Benjamin ran down the street, he wondered what he should buy. Should he buy candy? He hardly knew how it tasted. Should he buy a pretty toy? If he had been the only child in the family, things might have been different. But there were fourteen boys and girls older than he, and two little sisters who were younger.

What a big family it was! And the father was a poor man. No wonder the lad had never owned a toy.

He had not gone far when he met a larger boy, who was blowing a whistle.

"I wish I had that whistle," he said.

The big boy looked at him and blew it again. Oh, what a pretty sound it made!

"I have some pennies," said Benjamin. He held them in his hand, and showed them to the boy. "You may have them, if you will give me the whistle." "All of them?"

"Yes, all of them."

"Well, it's a bargain," said the boy; and he gave the whistle to

Benjamin, and took the pennies.

Little Benjamin Franklin was very happy; for he was only seven years old. He ran home as fast as he could, blowing the whistle as he ran.

"See, mother," he said, "I have bought a whistle."

"How much did you pay for it?"

"All the pennies you gave me."

"Oh, Benjamin!"

One of his brothers asked to see the whistle.

"Well, well!" he said. "You've paid a dear price for this thing. It's only a penny whistle, and a poor one at that."

WEEK 2 DAY 2 READING PASSAGE SUFFIXES

1. What are two specific reasons Benjamin Franklin's mother cannot give him more money in the story?

2. Describe the boy who sells Benjamin the whistle:

3. Which of these words with a suffix describes how Benjamin Franklin was before his mother gave him the pennies?

   A. Wealthiness
   B. Penniless
   C. Whistling
   D. Freedom

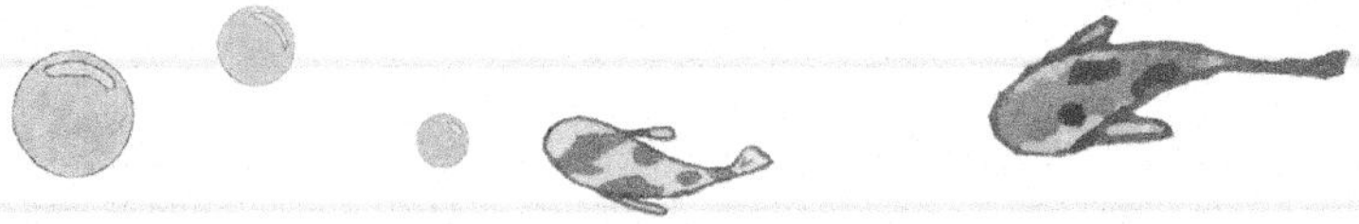

4. Which of these words from the passage describes how Benjamin Franklin's brother feels after he shows him the whistle?

   A. Hugable
   B. Punisher
   C. Regretful
   D. Mocking

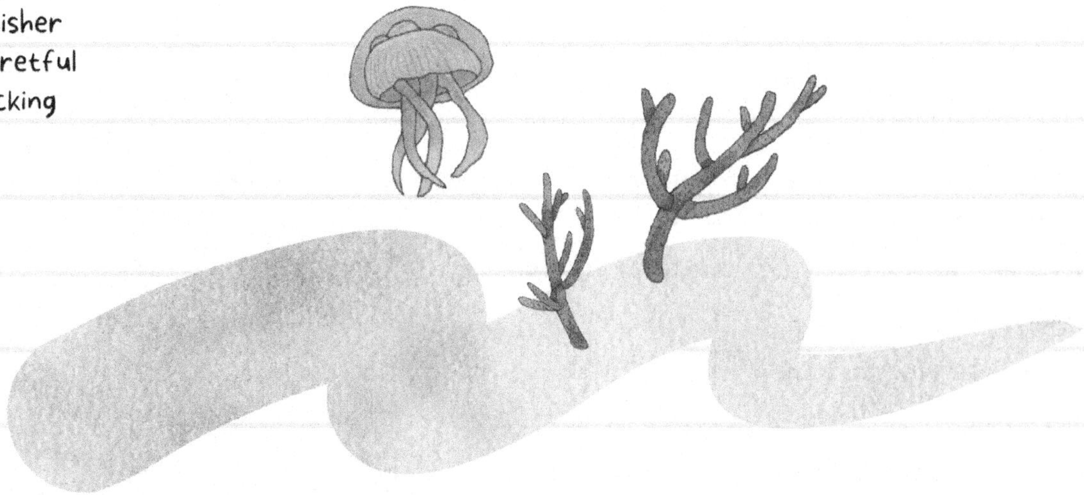

5. Why was it a mistake for Benjamin Franklin to buy that particular whistle?

⭐ **Directions:**

Fill in the blank by adding one of the Common Suffixes to the word in parentheses at the end of the sentence. Be sure to reread the sentence with your new word in place to make sure it makes sense!

1. People with upbeat personalities just seem to be _____ all the time. (JOY)

2. There are several different religious groups in India, but the largest one is _____. (HINDU)

3. After being famous for many years, many celebrities lose interest in their _____. (STAR)

4. Mail carriers always have to double-check to make sure they are delivering letters to the correct _____. (ADDRESS)

5. Our soccer team played with a lot of heart this year, but we were _____ because all the other teams in the league were so good. (WIN)

FITNESS

Please be aware of your environment and be safe at all times. If you cannot do an exercise, just try your best.

Repeat these **exercises 3 ROUNDS**

2 - Side Bending: 5 times to each side. Note: try to touch your feet.

1 - Squats: 5 times. Note: imagine you are trying to sit on a chair.

3 - Tree Pose: Stay as long as possible. Note: do the same with the other leg.

Diagrams: add/subtract/multiply/divide

1. Which equation does the number line most likely represent?

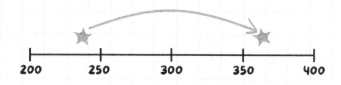

200   250   300   350   400

    A. 200 + 350 = 550
    B. 240 + 125 = 365
    C. 250 + 100 = 350
    D. 365 - 240 = 125

2. What is the difference between 48 - 21?

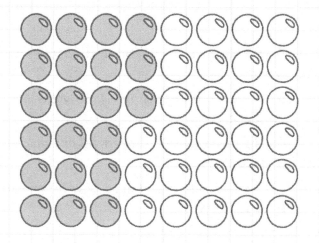

    A. 24
    B. 25
    C. 26
    D. 27

3. What is 7 x 14?

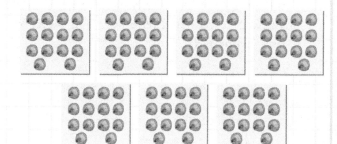

    A. 78
    B. 88
    C. 98
    D. 108

4. Which expression best represents the model below?

    A. 3 + 5
    B. 15 ÷ 5
    C. 15 - 3
    D. 15 - 5

5. Which equation does the number line most likely represent?

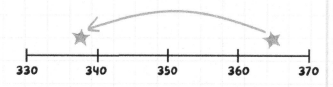

330   340   350   360   370

    A. 370 - 335 = 35
    B. 370 - 30 = 40
    C. 365 - 27 = 338
    D. 340 + 27 = 367

6. What is  ?

Each ⊚ has a value of 10.

Answer _____

7. A captain of a spacecraft has 36 buttons on the control panel. Which picture could represent how the buttons are arranged?

1

2

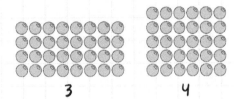

3   4

A. Diagram 1
B. Diagram 2
C. Diagram 3
D. Diagram 4

8. Which expression best represents the action on the number line below?

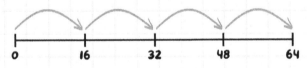

0   16   32   48   64

A. 16 × 4
B. 16 + 16 + 16
C. 16 + 4
D. 0 + 16

9. Which expression could represent the picture bellow?

A. 6 × 6 = 36
B. 6 + 7 = 13
C. 42 ÷ 7 = 6
D. 13 - 6 = 7

10. Which situation could be represented by the picture below?

A. 8 classmates each bring 8 pastries to share.

B. 8 classmates each bring 48 pastries to share.

C. 48 pastries are shared equally among 6 classmates.

D. 48 pastries are shared equally among 8 classmates.

Diagrams: add/subtract/multiply/divide

1. What is 8 multiplied by 4?

Answer _____

2. Which equation does the number line most likely represent?

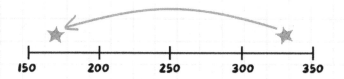

| 150 | 200 | 250 | 300 | 350 |

A. 170 + 250 = 420
B. 350 - 200 = 150
C. 330 - 160 = 170
D. 360 - 180 = 180

3. Which expression best represents the action on the number line below?

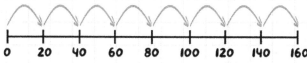

| 0 | 20 | 40 | 60 | 80 | 100 | 120 | 140 | 160 |

A. 20 + 8
B. 20 × 8
C. 0 + 160
D. 100 + 60

4. What is 240 subtracted from 1,000? Use 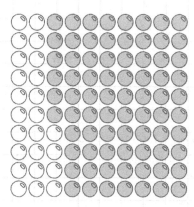 as 10.

Answer _____

5. Which situation could be represented by the picture below?

A. 72 crabs are shared equally among 8 men.

B. 9 men each caught and brought 9 crabs to share.

C. 9 men each caught and brought 72 crabs to share.

D. 72 crabs are shared equally among 9 men.

6. Which expression does the number line most likely represent?

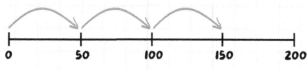

| 0 | 50 | 100 | 150 | 200 |

A. 0 + 150
B. 50 × 3
C. 100 + 50
D. 50 × 100

7. What is the value of the diagram below if one equals 70?

Answer _____

8. Which expression best represents the model below? Use as 10.

A. 240 ÷ 4
B. 240 ÷ 40
C. 24 ÷ 60
D. 240 ÷ 6

9. An astronaut has **56** packs of food in the box. Which picture could represent how the packs are arranged?

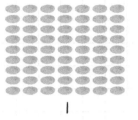

1   2

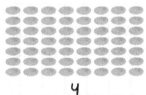

3   4

A. Diagram 1
B. Diagram 2
C. Diagram 3
D. Diagram 4

10. Which expression could represent the picture bellow? Use as 5.

A. 50 + 4
B. 5 x 4
C. 50 x 4
D. 25 x 4

FITNESS

Please be aware of your environment and be safe at all times. If you cannot do an exercise, just try your best.

Repeat these **exercises 3 ROUNDS**

1 - High Plank: 6 sec.

2 - Chair: 10 sec.
Note: sit on an imaginary chair, keep your back straight.

3 - Waist Hooping: 10 times.
Note: if you do not have a hoop, pretend you have an imaginary hoop and rotate your hips 10 times.

4 - Abs: 10 times

WEEK 2 DAY 5 MATH

Place Value

1. What is the tens place digit in the number 1,038?

   Answer _____

2. In the number 873 the number 8 is in what place value?

   Answer _____

3. How many times less is the digit 3 than the number 300?

   Answer _____

4. The ones place value digit in the number 1,783 is:

   Answer _____

5. In what place value is 2 in the number 2,174?

   A. Ones
   B. Tens
   C. Hundreds
   D. Thousands

6. Which digit represents the hundreds place in the number 1,642?

   A. 1
   B. 2
   C. 4
   D. 6

7. In which of the following numbers is the digit 3 in the greatest place value?

   A. 3,176
   B. 1,639
   C. 2,375
   D. 1,893

8. Ann wrote a number in which the digit 1 is in the greatest place value. Which number did she write?

   A. 2,981
   B. 2,176
   C. 1,234
   D. 3,314

9. The ones place value in the number 4,613 is:

   Answer _____

10. There are 5 ones, 7 hundreds, 2 tens and 3 thousands in the number thought by Jake. What is the number?

    A. 5,372
    B. 3,725
    C. 7,253
    D. 2,537

Standard form vs expanded form

1. Choose the option in which the number 932 is represented in an expanded form.

   A. 90 + 32
   B. 30 + 900 + 2
   C. 300 + 90 + 2
   D. 2 + 32 + 900

2. Which of the following answer choices represents the number one thousand, two hundred and seventy-six in standard form?

   A. 2,762
   B. 6,267
   C. 1,276
   D. 7,621

3. Choose the standard form of the number 5 + 800 + 40.

   A. 8,405
   B. 8,450
   C. 8,045
   D. 845

4. The number 735 in expanded form can be written as:

   A. 700 + 300 + 5
   B. 30 + 700 + 5
   C. 5 + 30 + 70
   D. 730 + 30 + 5

5. Choose the standard form of the number 300 + 8 + 50 + 1,000.

   A. 1,358
   B. 3,158
   C. 8,531
   D. 1,385

6. Write the number three thousand, six hundred and twenty-two in standard form.

   Answer _____

7. Write 8,563 in words.

   Answer _____

   _____

8. What is 50+7,000+4+300 in standard form?

   Answer _____

9. Write the expanded form of the number 2,739 in digits.

   Answer _____

10. What is 8 tens + 4 thousands + 6 ones + 5 hundreds in standard form?

    Answer _____

YOGA

Please be aware of your environment and be safe at all times. If you cannot do an exercise, just try your best.

1 - Down Dog: 10 sec.

2 - Bend Down: 10 sec.

3 - Chair: 10 sec.

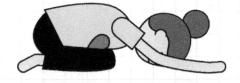

4 - Child Pose: 20 sec.

5 - Shavasana: as long as you can. Note: think of happy moments and relax your mind.

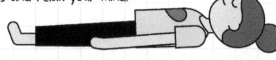

WEEK 2 DAY 6 🐟 EXPERIMENT

Racing With Mass

Last week, we introduced the concept of mass and created a balance to help us compare masses. This week, we'll start to look at how the mass of an object affects its ability to move by creating a racetrack! First, we'll build the track, then we'll time our race.

Materials:

🐟 Your balance (See last week's experiment)

🐟 A large, flattened cardboard box

🐟 A ruler or tape measure

🐟 Scissors or a box cutter (be sure to always have an adult help when you use sharp tools!)

🐟 Heavy tape, such as duct tape

🐟 A stop watch or timer

🐟 Several small balls (like golf balls, ping pong balls, marbles, etc.) that fit into the cups on your balance

Procedure:

1. Using your balance, compare the masses of the small balls or spheres you gathered. Using some note paper, rank them from highest mass to lowest mass. Set that information aside.

2. Using the ruler and a black marker, draw three rectangles that are at least **2** feet, **6** inches long and about three inches wide. It's important that all three rectangles are the same size!

3. Ask an adult to help you cut out the three rectangles you just created

4. Using your heavy tape, attach the three rectangles of cardboard to each other so they make a U-shaped trough that looks a little like a rain gutter. This is your racetrack!

5. Prop your completed racetrack against the edge of a sofa, coffee table, or other piece of furniture so that it looks like a ramp with a nice, gradual slope.

6. Gather your timer and the small spheres you compared earlier. One at a time, drop the spheres (don't push or force them!) into the top of the track you've created and measure how long it takes them to reach the floor using the stopwatch. Record this data on the same note paper you used to rank the masses of the objects earlier.

7. Once you've carried out this experiment and answered the follow-up questions below, be sure you save your ramp and your notes, as well as your balance for future experiments!

Follow-Up Questions:

1. What relationship did you notice between the mass of an object and the time it took it to go down the ramp?

2. Was there a certain object you thought would be faster or slower than it wound up being? Which object was it, and why were you surprised?

YOGA

Please be aware of your environment and be safe at all times. If you cannot do an exercise, just try your best.

1 - Tree Pose: Stay as long as possible. Note: do on one leg then on another.

2 - Down Dog: 10 sec.

3 - Stretching: Stay as long as possible. Note: do on one leg then on another.

6 - Shavasana: 5 min. Note: this pose is very important and provides you with long term benefits. Try not to skip this. Close your eyes and imagine who you want to be and what your goals are! Always think happy thoughts.

4 - Lower Plank: 6 sec. Note: Keep your back straight and body tight.

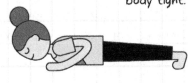

5 - Book Pose: 6 sec. Note: Keep your core tight. Legs should be across from your eyes.

Task: Yikes! All the snakes are tangled up. Go ahead and match the corresponding letters with the numbers.

As you read increasingly complex texts, you'll encounter words whose definitions you might not know. Of course, a dictionary or internet search can be used to find a definition quickly, but here are some other strategies you can use to help determine the meanings of words as you read. These strategies can be helpful on tests or other situations when you can't use a dictionary.

Strategy 1: Context Clues

One of the best ways to figure out what a new word means is to study the other words in the sentence and paragraph around it. That extra context provides you with clues.

 For Example...

Sentence: The surgeon took the scalpel from the nurse and made an incision on the patient's chest in order to access his heart.

This sentence has two words that might be unfamiliar: scalpel and incision. However, if we have a good understanding of what's going on in the sentence, the meaning of both words is pretty obvious.

- We know a scalpel is something a surgeon (doctor) uses to access someone's heart.
- We know an incision is what the surgeon makes with the scalpel in order to access the heart.

So, based on those context clues, we can conclude that a scalpel is a knife used by a surgeon, while an incision is a cut made by a scalpel!

Strategy 2: Breaking a Word Down

If you see a big, complex word that you can tell has prefixes and suffixes attached to it, it can be useful to break the word into its parts to help you understand it better.

 For Example...

Sentence: A lot of people assume that living without hot water would be an unmanageable problem, but a shocking number of Americans live that way.

The word unmanageable looks like a monstrous cluster of letters, but let's break it down into a prefix, a root word, and a suffix:

Prefix: Un (not)

Root: manage (to deal with or handle something)

Suffix: able (to do something)

So, when we break the word into three parts, we see that **unmanageable** simply means something that's impossible to handle or deal with!

The Miser
By Aesop

One day, a rich, greedy old man sold all of his possessions, took all his money, and bought a huge gold nugget that represented all of his wealth. Instead of putting it in a vault or showing it off to people, though, the old miser dug a hole on the outskirts of town and buried the gold nugget there. Every day, he would visit the place where the gold was buried, just to be near it.

Eventually, the town where the miser lived began expanding, and a construction crew that was building new houses on what had been the outskirts of town noticed the old man visiting the same spot every day. Eventually they got curious, and when they noticed that the ground had been dug up there at some point in the past, they dug down themselves and discovered the gold nugget, which they sold and split up the money.

The next day, the miser returned to his favorite place and was terrified to discover the empty hole. He began to cry and tear out his hair when one of the construction workers came over to console him.

"Look friend, I'll help you bury a rock in this hole to replace your lost gold. Then, each day, you can come here and know that there's something buried beneath your feet, just like you did before."

"What use will that be?" the old man whined. "A rock is not worth nearly as much as gold!"

"Your gold was of no value anyway," the worker told him, "because you refused to use it."

1. Based on the story, what does the word "Miser" mean?

2. Why does the construction worker say the gold was "of no value anyway?"

3. Which word does the phrase "...the town where the miser lived began expanding..." help the reader understand better?

A. Outskirts (Paragraph 1)
B. Construction (Paragraph 2)
C. Miser (Paragraph 1)
D. Terrified (Paragraph 3)

4. How did the miser's own behavior directly contribute to his loss?

A. He invested all of his wealth into one item.
B. He didn't understand that the gold had no real value because he wouldn't spend it.
C. The construction workers only got curious about the gold because he kept visiting it.
D. If he had hidden the gold better, nobody would have found it.

5. Why do you think the miser put all his wealth into one gold nugget and buried it in the first place?

Defining New Words with Context Clues

⭐ **Directions:**

Write a definition for the bold word or words in the sentence on the line below and circle the other words in the sentence that helped you come up with that definition..

1. The magician showed off his skill in **prestidigitation** by doing a variety of card tricks and pulling a rabbit out of a hat.

2. All the teachers and students had to go to the assembly hall for a **convocation** at the beginning of the school year.

3. Mr. Lawrence was awarded a medal for his bravery during the house fire, which is the highest **accolade** he has earned so far.

4. Charlie held back his tears and tried to be **stoic** when he fell, even though his knee was hurting very badly.

5. The students were filled with **ennui** because there was an hour left in the school day, and the teacher had said the only things they could do were read silently or do math problems.

FITNESS

Please be aware of your environment and be safe at all times. If you cannot do an exercise, just try your best.

1 - Abs: 3 times

Repeat these exercises **3 ROUNDS**

2 - Lunges: 2 times to each leg.
Note: Use your body weight or books as weight to do leg lunges.

4 - Run: 50m
Note: Run 25 meters to one side and 25 meters back to the starting position.

3 - Plank: 6 sec.

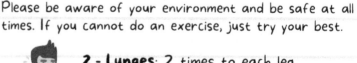

Speaking a Piece
By James Baldwin

Two children, brother and sister, were on their way to school. Both were very small. The boy was only four years old, and the girl was not yet six. "Come, Edward, we must hurry," said the sister. "We must not be late." With one hand the little boy clung to his sister's arm, and with the other he held his primer.

This primer was his only book, and he loved it. It had a bright blue cover, which he was careful not to soil. And in it were some odd little pictures, which he never grew tired of looking at.

Edward could spell nearly all the words in his primer, and he could read quite well.

The school was more than a mile from their home, and the children trotted along as fast as their short legs could carry them.

At a place where two roads crossed, they saw a tall gentleman coming to meet them. He was dressed in black, and had a very pleasant face.

"Oh, Edward, there is Mr. Harris!" whispered the little girl. "Don't forget your manners."

They were glad to see Mr. Harris, for he was the minister. They stopped by the side of the road and made their manners. Edward bowed very gracefully, and his sister curtsied.

"Good morning, children!" said the minister; and he kindly shook hands with both.

"I have something here for little Edward," he said. Then he took from his pocket a sheet of paper on which some verses were written.

"See! It is a little speech that I have written for him. The teacher will soon ask him to speak a piece at school, and I am sure that he can learn this easily and speak it well."

Edward took the paper and thanked the kind minister.

"Mother will help him learn it," said his sister.

"Yes, I will try to learn it," said Edward.

"Do so, my child," said the Minister; "and I hope that when you grow up you will become a wise man and a great orator."

Then the two children hurried on to school.

The speech was not hard to learn, and Edward soon knew every word of it. When the time came for him to speak, his mother and the minister were both there to hear him.

He spoke so well that everybody was pleased. He pronounced every word plainly, as though he were talking to his schoolmates.

I. Write down **four different words** from the story that helped you understand that a "primer" is a kind of book.

2. What details from the passage tell you that, in the world of the text, a "minister" is a highly respected person?

3. Based on the passage, which of these words do you think is the closest in meaning to **"curtsied?"**

    A. Whispered (Paragraph 6)
    B. Stopped (Paragraph 7)
    C. Bowed (Paragraph 7)
    D. Took (Paragraph 9)

4. What detail from earlier in the text predicted that Edward would be good at learning the piece Mr. Harris gave him?

    A. Earlier in the story, it said that Edward was very good at reading, even though he was only four.
    B. Earlier in the story, it said that Mr. Harris was a respected person, so Edward would want to impress him.
    C. Earlier in the story, it said that Edward was the best student in his class.
    D. Earlier in the story, it said that Edward had good manners.

5. Based on the passage, what do you think it means to **"speak a piece?"**

Defining New Words by Breaking Them Down

⭐ **Directions:**

In the space below each sentence, break each word down into its parts: prefix, root word, and suffix. Then, write a definition for the word based on your breakdown

1. Unfortunately, our concert tickets were **nonrefundable**, which meant we couldn't get our money back when it rained.

Prefix: _____

Root Word: _____

Suffix: _____

Definition: _____

2. The word "car" is much less impressive than "automobile."

Prefix: _____

Root Word: _____

Definition: _____

3. The county judge is an appointee of the governor.

Root Word: _____

Suffix: _____

Definition: _____

4. The cornfield was a dry, yellow-brown color and dotted only with postharvest stubble from what had been corn stalks.

Prefix: ~~~~~~

Root Word: ~~~~~~

Definition: ~~~~~~

5. My uncle doesn't believe in giving fancy presents or buying the newest technology gadgets because he believes in anticonsumerism.

Prefix: ~~~~~~

Root Word: ~~~~~~

Suffix: ~~~~~~

Definition: ~~~~~~

FITNESS

Please be aware of your environment and be safe at all times. If you cannot do an exercise, just try your best.

Repeat these **exercises 3 ROUNDS**

3 - Abs: 10 times

4 - High Plank: 6 sec.

1 - Squats: 5 times. Note: imagine you are trying to sit on a chair.

2 - Side Bending: 5 times to each side. Note: try to touch your feet.

5 - Tree Pose: Stay as long as possible. Note: do the same with the other leg.

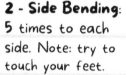

WEEK 3 DAY 3 🐋 MATH

Rounding to nearest 10, 100 and 1,000

1. What is 679 rounded to the nearest hundred?

   A. 670
   B. 680
   C. 600
   D. 700

2. Round 837 to the nearest ten.

   A. 830
   B. 840
   C. 800
   D. 900

3. What is 1,056 rounded to the nearest thousand?

   A. 1,050
   B. 1,100
   C. 1,000
   D. 1,156

4. Which of the following numbers rounded to the nearest hundred gives you 800?

   A. 784
   B. 853
   C. 745
   D. 739

5. Which of the following numbers rounded to the nearest hundred gives you 1,000?

   A. 923
   B. 1,562
   C. 976
   D. 943

6. Round 673 to the nearest ten.

   Answer _____

7. Round 2,359 to the nearest thousand.

   Answer _____

8. Which place value do you need to round in the number 4,736 to get 4,700?

   Answer _____

9. Round 835 and 832 to the nearest ten. Write a number sentence using those two rounded numbers and a comparison symbol.

   Answer _____

10. What is 3,995 rounded to the nearest ten?

    Answer _____

Fraction Comparison Problems

1. Which number sentence below is true?

   A. $\frac{1}{2} = \frac{3}{8}$

   B. $\frac{3}{4} < \frac{3}{5}$

   C. $\frac{2}{3} > \frac{2}{4}$

   D. $\frac{6}{1} < 5$

2. Which expression could represent the picture below?

A. $\frac{3}{4} = \frac{2}{4}$

B. $\frac{3}{4} < \frac{2}{4}$

C. $\frac{3}{4} > \frac{2}{4}$

D. $\frac{3}{4} = \frac{1}{4}$

3. Which fraction can be used to make the number sentence true?

$$\text{-----} > \frac{4}{8}$$

A. $\frac{5}{6}$

B. $\frac{3}{9}$

C. $\frac{2}{5}$

D. $\frac{3}{7}$

4. Ian drank $\frac{2}{4}$ of his orange juice and Becky drank $\frac{1}{2}$ of hers. Which statement is true?

A. $\frac{2}{4} > \frac{1}{2}$

B. $\frac{2}{4} < \frac{1}{2}$

C. $\frac{2}{4} = \frac{1}{2}$

D. $\frac{2}{4} \neq \frac{1}{2}$

5. Find the fraction that makes the number sentence true.

$$\frac{4}{8} < \text{----}$$

A. $\frac{3}{8}$

B. $\frac{3}{4}$

C. $\frac{1}{2}$

D. $\frac{1}{4}$

FITNESS

Repeat these exercises 3 ROUNDS

Please be aware of your environment and be safe at all times. If you cannot do an exercise, just try your best.

1 - Bend forward: 10 times.
Note: try to touch your feet. Make sure to keep your back straight and if needed you can bend your knees.

2 - Lunges: 3 times to each leg.
Note: Use your body weight or books as weight to do leg lunges.

3 - Plank: 6 sec.

4 - Abs: 10 times

Fraction Comparison Problems

1. Compare $\frac{1}{3}$ and $\frac{2}{4}$ using a comparison symbol.

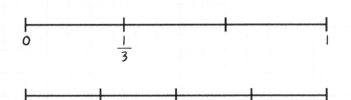

Answer _____

2. Put $\frac{4}{10}$, $\frac{1}{2}$, $\frac{3}{5}$ on the number line.

3. Complete the equation $7 = \frac{7}{?}$

Answer _____

4. A captain eats $\frac{1}{2}$ plate of rice and $\frac{2}{3}$ cup of tea. Which statement is true?

A. $\frac{1}{2} > \frac{2}{3}$

B. $\frac{1}{2} < \frac{2}{3}$

C. $\frac{1}{2} = \frac{2}{3}$

D. $\frac{2}{3} < \frac{1}{2}$

5. Compare $\frac{5}{6}$ and $\frac{2}{3}$ using a comparison symbol.

Fractions with diagrams

1. What fraction is represented by the model below?

A. $\frac{3}{4}$

B. $\frac{8}{3}$

C. $\frac{3}{8}$

D. $\frac{4}{3}$

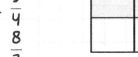

2. Which fraction shows the shaded portion for the model below?

A. $\frac{1}{4}$ or one half

B. $\frac{4}{16}$ or one half

C. $\frac{1}{16}$ or one fourths

D. $\frac{4}{16}$ or one fourths

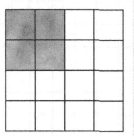

3. Which of the following pictures represents four-sixths?

A.

B.

C.

D.

4. What is the fraction that represents the UNSHADED portion in the model below?

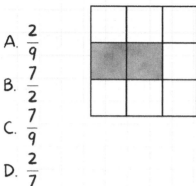

A. $\frac{2}{9}$

B. $\frac{7}{2}$

C. $\frac{7}{9}$

D. $\frac{2}{7}$

5. Using the model below, which number sentence is FALSE?

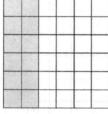

A. $\frac{12}{36} = \frac{3}{9}$

B. $\frac{12}{36} = \frac{1}{3}$

C. $\frac{3}{9} = \frac{1}{3}$

D. $\frac{6}{36} = \frac{3}{9}$

6. Write a statement represented by the model below.

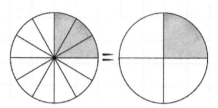

Answer _____

7. Write in the missing fraction for the number line below.

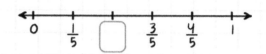

Answer _____

8. Write a fraction to represent the shaded portion for the model below.

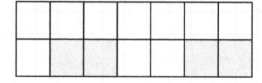

Answer _____

FITNESS

Please be aware of your environment and be safe at all times. If you cannot do an exercise, just try your best.

Repeat these **exercises 3 ROUNDS**

1 - High Plank: 6 sec.

2 - Chair: 10 sec. Note: sit on an imaginary chair, keep your back straight.

3 - Waist Hooping: 10 times. Note: if you do not have a hoop, pretend you have an imaginary hoop and rotate your hips 10 times.

4 - Abs: 10 times

Fractions with diagrams

1. Which fractions are missing from the number line below?

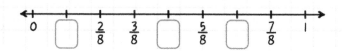

Answer _____

2. Complete the statement represented by the model below.

$$\frac{?}{15} = \frac{2}{?}$$ =

Answer _____

Fractions: add/subtract and multiply (Same denominator)

1. Using the model below, which number sentence is true?

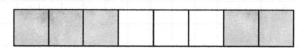

A. $\frac{1}{8} + \frac{1}{8} + \frac{1}{8} = \frac{2}{8}$

B. $\frac{1}{8} + \frac{1}{8} + \frac{1}{8} = \frac{3}{8}$

C. $\frac{3}{8} + \frac{2}{8} = \frac{5}{8}$

D. $\frac{3}{8} + \frac{3}{8} = \frac{2}{8}$

2. What is the sum of $\frac{2}{6}$ and $\frac{3}{6}$?

A. $\frac{5}{12}$

B. $\frac{5}{6}$

C. $\frac{23}{66}$

D. $\frac{6}{36}$

3. Use the model below to find $\frac{2}{9} \times 3$.

A. $\frac{6}{9}$

B. $\frac{6}{27}$

C. $\frac{6}{18}$

D. $\frac{3}{9}$

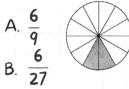

4. What is $\frac{5}{6} - \frac{3}{6}$?

A. $\frac{3}{6}$

B. $\frac{1}{6}$

C. $\frac{2}{6}$

D. $\frac{4}{6}$

5. What is $\frac{5}{14}$ subtracted from $\frac{12}{14}$?

A. $\frac{2}{14}$

B. $\frac{6}{14}$

C. $\frac{5}{14}$

D. $\frac{7}{14}$

6. Which number sentence is modeled below?

A. $\dfrac{1}{12} \times 4 = \dfrac{4}{12}$

B. $\dfrac{3}{12} \times 4 = \dfrac{12}{12}$

C. $\dfrac{3}{6} \times 4 = \dfrac{12}{6}$

D. $\dfrac{4}{12} \times 3 = \dfrac{12}{12}$

7. Write a subtraction statement represented by the model below.

$$\dfrac{6}{10} - \dfrac{?}{10} = \dfrac{2}{10}$$

Answer _____

8. What is another way to write
$$\dfrac{1}{8} + \dfrac{1}{8} + \dfrac{1}{8} + \dfrac{1}{8} + \dfrac{1}{8}?$$

Answer _____

9. Find $3 \times \dfrac{2}{7}$.

Answer _____

10. What is $\dfrac{3}{9}$ added to $\dfrac{1}{9}$ and then multiplied by 2?

Answer _____

YOGA

Please be aware of your environment and be safe at all times. If you cannot do an exercise, just try your best.

1 - Down Dog: 10 sec.

2 - Bend Down: 10 sec.

3 - Chair: 10 sec.

4 - Child Pose: 20 sec.

5 - Shavasana: as long as you can. Note: think of happy moments and relax your mind.

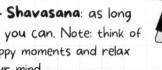

WEEK 3 DAY 6 🐋 EXPERIMENT

How Force Affects Motion

This week, we'll be using our balance and racetrack to continue building an understanding of how mass, motion, and force are related. Force is a push or pull that affects an object's motion.

Materials:

- 🐟 Your balance (See last Week 1's experiment)
- 🐟 Your racetrack (See Week 2's experiment)
- 🐟 A ruler or tape measure
- 🐟 A stop watch or timer
- 🐟 Several small balls (like golf balls, ping pong balls, marbles, etc.) that fit into the cups on your balance
- 🐟 Your notes from Week 2's experiment

Procedure:

1. Using your balance, compare the masses of the small balls or spheres you gathered. Using some note paper, rank them from highest mass to lowest mass. Set that information aside. (NOTE: If you're using the same objects you did last week and you still have your notes, you can skip this step and just review what you already have written down.)

2. Set up your racetrack like you did last week and practice placing balls at the top of the ramp and giving them a push. Last week, we were just dropping objects into the ramp, but this time, we want to put a little force behind them. Your goal is to make the amount of force you're giving with each push the same. Practice giving the objects a "little push" and a "big push."

3. Gather your timer and the small spheres you compared earlier, and one at a time, place the spheres into the top of the track you've created and give them a little push down the ramp. Using the stopwatch, measure how long it takes them to reach the floor. Record this data on the same note paper you used to rank the masses of the objects earlier (and, ideally, the times you recorded last week).

4. After you've recorded all your "little push" times, it's time for the big push! Place each object at the top of the ramp, give it a big push down, and record the time.

5. After you've done two runs for all your spheres (a little push run and a big push run), take a look at your notes and answer the questions below.

6. Be sure to save your balance, your racetrack, and your notes for next week's experiment!

Follow-Up Questions:

1. How do the times for the pushed objects compare to the times for the dropped objects (last week)?

_____

_____

_____

2. How did the mass of the object seem to change the way your pushes affected the time?

_____

_____

_____

YOGA

Please be aware of your environment and be safe at all times. If you cannot do an exercise, just try your best.

1 - Tree Pose:
Stay as long as possible.
Note: do on one leg then on another.

2 - Down Dog: 10 sec.

3 - Stretching:
Stay as long as possible. Note: do on one leg then on another.

6 - Shavasana: 5 min.
Note: this pose is very important and provides you with long term benefits. Try not to skip this. Close your eyes and imagine who you want to be and what your goals are! Always think happy thoughts.

4 - Lower Plank: 6 sec.
Note: Keep your back straight and body tight.

5 - Book Pose: 6 sec.
Note: Keep your core tight. Legs should be across from your eyes.

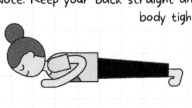

Task: Looks like the cassete tapes have been tangled up. Find the cassete tape that is connected to the cassete player.

Keep at it!

This week we will learn about commonly confused words, talk about fractions, and learn about friction.

WEEK 4

It's a seahorse!

Did you know seahorses do not have teeth or a stomach? Since seahorses do not have a stomach, they must eat often to stay alive.

ARGOPREP

Written English can be complex because there are a lot of words that sound the same when we speak, but actually have totally different meanings on the page. When two words with different meanings sound the same, we call them homonyms. If two homonyms are spelled differently in writing, we call those homophones.

When we write, it's really important to pay attention to words that have homophones so we can be sure to choose the right spelling.

 ## Key Terms

Homonyms: Words that sound the same when spoken

Homophones: Words that sound the same when spoken, but have different definitions and different spellings

NOTE: All homophones are homonyms. **Not** all homonyms are homophones!

 ## For Example...

Sentence 1: My aunt and uncle are very proud of their new car.
Sentence 2: I think I left the ball over there, by the fence.

Their and there are homophones. They sound the same when you read the sentence out loud, but they have different spellings and unique meanings.

Sentence 1: Mrs. Fletcher bought two tickets to the baseball game.
Sentence 2: After I saw my sister with ice cream, I wanted dessert too!

Two and too are homophones. They sound the same when you read the sentence out loud, but they have different spellings and unique meanings.

Common Homophones:

Prefix	Definition	Example
There	A word that refers to a place, location, or direction	Look over there!
Their	A possessive pronoun that shows ownership	Sally and Steve are very proud of their house.
They're	A contraction (shortened form) of "They are"	I don't like hanging out with my cousins because they're always getting into trouble.
To	A word that usually refers to a direction something is moving or being given	1. I walked to school this morning. 2. I gave a toaster to Mom for her birthday.
Two	The number between one and three (2)	A bicycle has two wheels.
Too	Also or as well	I want cheesecake too!
Hole	An opening or hollow place	My dog keeps digging holes in the back yard.
Whole	All of something; the entirety of something	The whole class had lunch detention because nobody would admit to throwing the paper airplane.
It's	A contraction (shortened form) of "It is"	It's a beautiful day outside!
Its	A possessive pronoun that shows ownership	The squirrel waved its bushy tail in the air.

The Fox and the Woodcutter
By Aesop

One day, a fox was minding its own business in the woods when a pack of hounds belonging to some hunters discovered it and began to give chase. The fox had heard the clumsy hounds coming from a mile away and gotten a head start, but it knew that if it couldn't find shelter, the hounds would eventually catch up to him or, worse yet, the hunters might appear.

The fox ran into a woodcutter, who was chopping down a tree for firewood. The fox begged the woodsman for help, promising him that he'd find a way to repay the favor somehow. The woodcutter agreed to protect the fox and brought him back to his hut, where he hid him in a corner behind some boxes and blankets.

Eventually, the hounds led the hunters to the woodcutter's house, and the hunters knocked on the door to ask if he had seen a fox.

"No, I haven't seen any fox," the woodcutter said, although he pointed to the corner where the fox was hiding as he said it. "No foxes have come through here at all. There definitely aren't any foxes in my hut right now," he repeated, pointing violently toward the spot where there was a fox in the hut.

Now, the fox was peering out through a small gap in the blankets that covered it in the corner, so it knew that the woodcutter had betrayed its trust. However, the hunters were too eager to catch the fox and failed to pick up on the woodsman s pointing. Instead, they took him at his word and left, continuing deeper into the woods to find the fox.

As soon as they were gone, the fox jumped out of the corner and ran for the door.

"Come back here, you ungrateful fox!" the woodcutter cried out. "You promised to repay me!"

"Repay you?" the fox called back. "I would have gladly repaid you if your actions were as good as your words," it said, bounding away to find another safe place.

1. What is the major conflict or problem the fox is dealing with in this story?

~~~~~~

~~~~~~

2. What would you say is the "moral" or "message" of this story? Why do you say that?

~~~~~~

~~~~~~

~~~~~~

~~~~~~

3. Which of these sentences correctly uses the word "its," as it is used in the sentence, "...so it knew that the woodcutter had betrayed its trust..."?

   A. Its a beautiful day outside!
   B. I can't eat ice cream because its too cold for my teeth.
   C. The fox wagged its tail with joy.
   D. I don't like to play outside when its too hot.

4. Which of these sentences correctly uses the word "there," as it is used in the sentence, "There definitely aren't any foxes in my hut right now?"

   A. My grandparents got a flat tire on there car.
   B. I don't like cats because there too private.
   C. Meet me there after school so we can study together.
   D. Teddy and Maria are hoping to improve there grades.

5. In your opinion, which character's actions in the story are the worst: the fox, the hunters, or the woodsman? Explain your choice.

Identifying Homophone Usage Errors

⭐ **Directions:**

Each sentence below contains a bold word which has potential homophones. On the line below the sentence, write whether the word is the Correct or Incorrect form. If the usage is wrong, write the correct form of the word on the line as well.

1. I love camping with my dad's family because **their** all very passionate about the outdoors.

2. I swear my printer has a life of **it's** own: every time I change the paper, it just jams!

3. For **our** vacation, my family and I are traveling to Houston, Texas.

4. I ate a **hole** apple, including the stem and seeds, which made me feel sick.

5. I started the day off with **too** pencils, but now I can't find either one of them.

FITNESS

Please be aware of your environment and be safe at all times. If you cannot do an exercise, just try your best.

Repeat these **exercises 3 ROUNDS**

1 - Abs: 3 times

2 - Lunges: 2 times to each leg.
Note: Use your body weight or books as weight to do leg lunges.

4 - Run: 50m
Note: Run 25 meters to one side and 25 meters back to the starting position.

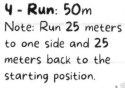

3 - Plank: 6 sec.

The Ettrick Shepherd
By James Baldwin

In Scotland there once lived a poor shepherd whose name was James Hogg. His father and grandfather and great-grandfather had all been shepherds.

It was his business to take care of the sheep which belonged to a rich landholder by the Ettrick Water. Sometimes he had several hundreds of lambs to look after. He drove these to the pastures on the hills and watched them day after day while they fed on the short green grass.

He had a dog which he called Sirrah. This dog helped him watch the sheep. He would drive them from place to place as his master wished. Sometimes he would take care of the whole flock while the shepherd was resting or eating his dinner.

One dark night James Hogg was on the hilltop with a flock of seven hundred lambs. Sirrah was with him. Suddenly a storm came up. There was thunder and lightning; the wind blew hard; the rain poured.

The poor lambs were frightened. The shepherd and his dog could not keep them together. Some of them ran towards the east, some towards the west, and some towards the south.

The shepherd soon lost sight of them in the darkness. With his lighted lantern in his hand, he went up and down the rough hills calling for his lambs.

Two or three other shepherds joined him in the search. All night long they sought for the lambs.

Morning came and still they sought. They looked, as they thought, in every place where the lambs might have taken shelter.

At last James Hogg said, "It's of no use; all we can do is to go home and tell the master that we have lost his whole flock."

They had walked a mile or two towards home, when they came to the edge of a narrow and deep ravine. They looked down, and at the bottom they saw some lambs huddled together among the rocks. And there was Sirrah standing guard over them and looking all around for help "These must be the lambs that rushed off towards the south," said James Hogg.

The men hurried down and soon saw that the flock was a large one.

"I really believe they are all here," said one.

They counted them and were surprised to find that not one lamb of the great flock of seven hundred was missing.

How had Sirrah managed to get the three scattered divisions together? How had he managed to drive all the frightened little animals into this place of safety?

Nobody could answer these questions. But there was no shepherd in

Scotland that could have done better than Sirrah did that night.

1. Based on the passage, how would you describe James Hogg?

2. Why does the narrator say, "There was no shepherd in Scotland that could have done better than Sirrah did that night?"

3. Which of these sentences correctly uses the word "to," as it is used in the sentence, "...the sheep which belonged to a rich landholder."

   A. Cherry is my favorite flavor for popsicles, but I like watermelon to.
   B. I gave a big, red card to my mother on Valentine's Day.
   C. We only brought to bottles of water on an eight-mile hike.
   D. I wanted to go swimming on our vacation, but it was to rainy.

4. Which of these sentences correctly uses the word "there," as it is used in the sentence, "There was no shepherd in Scotland that could have done better than Sirrah..."

   A. Even though there annoying sometimes, I love my little cousins very much.
   B. When football players crash into each other, there heads can get injured badly.
   C. I think that there just jealous of us!
   D. We were delayed because there was a flock of turkeys blocking the road.

5. In your opinion, who is a more important character in this story: James Hogg or Sirrah the dog? What makes you say that?

Directions:

Fill in the blank by adding the correct word from the set of homophones in parentheses at the end of the sentence. Be sure to double-check the sentence with your new word in place to make sure it makes sense!

1. The sand at that beach is very rocky, so wear sandals when you walk _____. (THERE / THEIR / THEY'RE)

2. Suddenly, a _____ opened up in the middle of the intersection, causing cars to slam on their brakes. (WHOLE / HOLE)

3. In 1803, the French government sold over **800,000** square miles of land _____ the United States in what is now called "The Louisiana Purchase." (TWO / TO / TOO)

4. The wheelbarrow was useless because the wheel had broken off of _____ axel. (ITS / IT'S)

5. California is famous for _____ beautiful scenery and rich history. (ITS / IT'S)

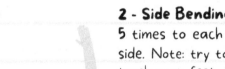

Repeat these exercises 3 ROUNDS

Please be aware of your environment and be safe at all times. If you cannot do an exercise, just try your best.

2 - Side Bending: 5 times to each side. Note: try to touch your feet.

3 - Tree Pose: Stay as long as possible. Note: do the same with the other leg.

1 - Squats: 5 times. Note: imagine you are trying to sit on a chair.

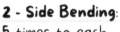

Shading in fraction models

1. Which fraction of the shape is shaded?

A. $\frac{3}{10}$

B. $\frac{3}{15}$

C. $\frac{1}{3}$

D. $\frac{12}{15}$

2. How can we calculate the shaded area?

Answer _____

3. What is $\frac{1}{5}$ subtracted from $\frac{4}{5}$?

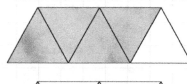

Answer _____

4. What fraction represents the shaded portion on the model below?

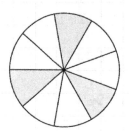

A. $\frac{3}{9}$

B. $\frac{6}{3}$

C. $\frac{3}{6}$

D. $\frac{6}{9}$

5. Write a fraction for the shaded portion for the model below.

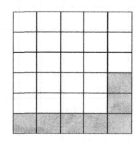

Answer _____

Comparing numbers using comparison symbols ($<$, $>$, $=$)

1. Which of the following number sentences is true?

   A. $579 < 581$
   B. $1,762 > 1,801$
   C. $349 = 359$
   D. $2,681 < 1,986$

2. Compare 984 and 976 using a comparison symbol.

   Answer _____

3. Which expression is true?

   A. 683 > 689
   B. 1,274 < 1,269
   C. 579 < 591
   D. 819 > 831

4. Compare 564 - 176 and 348 using a comparison symbol.

   Answer _____

5. Which symbol would make this inequality true?

   1,187 ____ 1,179

   A. >
   B. <
   C. =
   D. +

6. Which number sentence is true?

   A. 534 = 175 + 349
   B. 863 > 574 + 279
   C. 635 < 268 + 357
   D. 437 = 232 + 215

7. Compare the numbers 869 and 894 using a comparison symbol.

   Answer _____

8. What is the missing number?

   1,358 < _____

   A. 1,349
   B. 1,352
   C. 1,361
   D. 1,344

9. Compare the numbers 1,329 and 1,316 using a comparison symbol.

   Answer _____

10. Compare 456 + 138 and 256 + 338 using a comparison symbol.

    Answer _____

FITNESS

Repeat these exercises **3 ROUNDS**

Please be aware of your environment and be safe at all times. If you cannot do an exercise, just try your best.

1 - Bend forward: 10 times.
Note: try to touch your feet. Make sure to keep your back straight and if needed you can bend your knees.

2 - Lunges: 3 times to each leg.
Note: Use your body weight or books as weight to do leg lunges.

3 - Plank: 6 sec.

4 - Abs: 10 times

Area and perimeter

1. Find the perimeter of the shape below.

[rectangle: 23 in, 49 in]

A. 134 in
B. 144 in
C. 154 in
D. 164 in

2. Find the perimeter of the shape below.

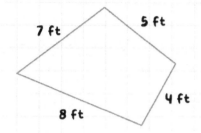

A. 24 ft
B. 25 ft
C. 28 ft
D. 29 ft

3. The perimeter of a square is 68 yards. What is the length of one of the sides?

Answer _____

4. A rectangle measures 8 inches in width. The length is 3 times as long as its width. Find the perimeter of the rectangle.

Answer _____

5. The perimeter of this quadrilateral is 72 yards. What is the value of k?

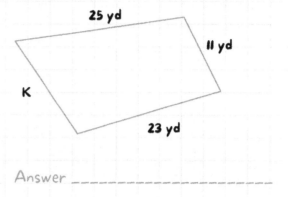

Answer _____

6. What is the area of this rectangle?

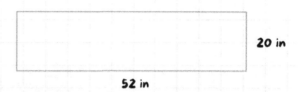

A. 1,020 sq in
B. 1,030 sq in
C. 1,040 sq in
D. 1,050 sq in

7. One side of a square is 8 feet long. What is its area?

A. 56 sq ft
B. 64 sq ft
C. 72 sq ft
D. 81 sq ft

8. What is the area of the shape below?

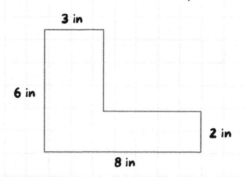

A. 24 sq in
B. 32 sq in
C. 22 sq in
D. 28 sq in

9. The model below represent sections that are covered with trees. The area of the entire model is 18 square yards. What is the total area of the trees (shaded portion) in square yards?

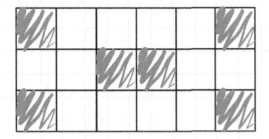

A. 12 sq yd
B. 4 sq yd
C. 6 sq yd
D. 2 sq yd

10. The area of a rectangle is 63 sq cm. The length is 9 cm. What is the width of the rectangle?

A. 6 cm
B. 7 cm
C. 8 cm
D. 9 cm

Identifying number patterns

1. The rule for the pattern shown below is "+ 3". Fill in the missing numbers.
3, 6, ..., 12, ..., 18

Answer _____

2. Tammy listed these numbers: 2, 6, 18, 54, 162. What rule did Tammy use?

A. Add 2
B. Add 3
C. Times 2
D. Times 3

3. The chart below shows how many comics James draws.

Monday	Tuesday	Wednesday
2	8	14

Thursday	Friday	Saturday
20	26	32

If the pattern continues, how many comics will James draw on Sunday?

A. 34 comics
B. 36 comics
C. 38 comics
D. 39 comics

Please be aware of your environment and be safe at all times. If you cannot do an exercise, just try your best.

FITNESS

Repeat these exercises **3 ROUNDS**

1 - High Plank: 6 sec.

2 - Chair: 10 sec.
Note: sit on an imaginary chair, keep your back straight.

3 - Waist Hooping: 10 times. Note: if you do not have a hoop, pretend you have an imaginary hoop and rotate your hips 10 times.

4 - Abs: 10 times

WEEK 4 DAY 5 🐟 MATH

Identifying number patterns

1. Look at the pattern below.

   A. What "rule" is being used?

   Answer _____

   B. What might the next shape look like?

   Answer _____

2. Willy recorded the hours he practiced math each week before the test. If this pattern continues, how many hours will he practice on Week 7?

Week 1	Week 2	Week 3
5	9	13

Week 4	Week 5
17	21

   A. 25 hours
   B. 27 hours
   C. 29 hours
   D. 31 hours

3. The number pattern is "times 7". Which number is after 1, 7, 49?

   A. 249
   B. 343
   C. 379
   D. 423

4. The rule for the pattern shown is "+ 12". Fill in the missing numbers.
   10, ..., 34, 46, ..., 70

   Answer _____

5. Which rule describes the pattern: 4, 19, 34, 49?

   Answer _____

6. If the rule is "times 2", which of these numbers could be in the pattern 3, 6, 12, ...?

   A. 88
   B. 86
   C. 94
   D. 96

7. The rule for the pattern shown below is "add 5". Fill in the missing numbers.
   12, ..., ..., 27, ..., 37.

   Answer _____

Tables/Charts and understanding data

Using the following chart, answer the question 1 - 2. The family went on a picnic and brought some sandwiches, apples and cartons of juice. They made a table of the food they brought:

Food	🥪	🍎	🧃
How many?	16	12	8

1. How many sandwiches did they bring?

   Answer _____

2. How many more apples than cartons of juice did they bring?

   A. 4
   B. 5
   C. 6
   D. 8

Use the following pictograph to answer question 3 - 4.

Favorite Animals in our Street

3. Which animal is the most popular in our Street?

    A. Cat
    B. Dog
    C. Rabbit
    D. They are all equal

4. How many more cats are favored than rabbits?

    Answer _____

Kellie went to local store and bought some oranges, cucumbers, eggs, and chocolate bars. Using the following chart, answer questions 5 - 6.

Food	🍊	🥒	🥚	🍫
How many?	16	22	12	4

5. Which item did Kellie buy the most?

    A. Oranges
    B. Cucumbers
    C. Eggs
    D. Chocolate bars

6. How many more oranges than eggs did she buy?

    A. 10
    B. 6
    C. 4
    D. 12

YOGA

Please be aware of your environment and be safe at all times. If you cannot do an exercise, just try your best.

1 - Down Dog: 10 sec.

2 - Bend Down: 10 sec.

3 - Chair: 10 sec.

4 - Child Pose: 20 sec.

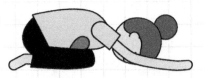

5 - Shavasana: as long as you can. Note: think of happy moments and relax your mind.

WEEK 4 DAY 6 🐟 EXPERIMENT

How Friction Affects Motion

This week, we'll be using our balance and racetrack to continue building an understanding of how mass, motion, force, and friction are related. Friction is the resistance you feel when you try to push a heavy object along the floor. Like mass and force, friction has a major impact on motion!

Materials:

- 🐟 Your balance (See last Week 1's experiment)
- 🐟 Your racetrack (See Week 2's experiment)
- 🐟 A stop watch or timer
- 🐟 Several small balls (like golf balls, ping pong balls, marbles, etc.) that fit into the cups on your balance
- 🐟 Your notes from Week 2 and Week 3's experiments
- 🐟 A few pieces of rough sandpaper
- 🐟 A few cotton balls
- 🐟 Tape
- 🐟 Scissors

Procedure:

1. Using your balance, compare the masses of the small balls or spheres you gathered. Using some note paper, rank them from highest mass to lowest mass. Set that information aside. (NOTE: If you're using the same objects you did last week and you still have your notes, you can skip this step and just review what you already have written down.)

2. Cut a few pieces of sandpaper that are the same width as the bottom of your track. Then, using the tape, place a few sections of sandpaper along the track. This will create some friction!

3. Take a few cotton balls and gently pull them apart so they create a spiderweb-like pad. Using the tape, attach a few fuzzy pieces of cotton ball along the track. This will create some more friction!

4. Set up your track so it's ready for racing. Gather your timer and the small spheres you compared earlier. One at a time, drop the spheres (don't push or force them!) into the top of the track you've created and measure how long it takes them to reach the floor using the stopwatch. Record this data on the same note paper you've been using the last two weeks.

5. Next, place the spheres into the top of the track one at a time and give them a little push down the ramp. Measure how long it takes them to reach the floor using the stopwatch. Record this data on your note paper.

6. After you've recorded all your "little push" times, it's time for the big push! Place each object at the top of the ramp, give it a big push down, and record the time.

7. After you've done three runs for all your spheres (a drop run, a little push run, and a big push run), take a look at your notes and answer the questions below.

8. Once you're done with this experiment, you should keep your racetrack, as we'll use it for some more experiments in the future.

Follow-Up Questions:

1. How did the mass of the spheres impact how much the friction slowed them down?

2. Did friction affect the dropped objects or the pushed objects more? Why do you think that was the case?

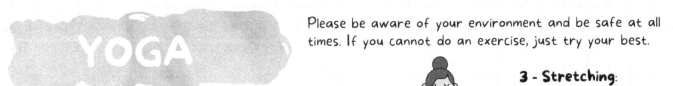

YOGA

Please be aware of your environment and be safe at all times. If you cannot do an exercise, just try your best.

1 - Tree Pose: Stay as long as possible. Note: do on one leg then on another.

2 - Down Dog: 10 sec.

3 - Stretching: Stay as long as possible. Note: do on one leg then on another.

4 - Lower Plank: 6 sec. Note: Keep your back straight and body tight.

5 - Book Pose: 6 sec. Note: Keep your core tight. Legs should be across from your eyes.

6 - Shavasana: 5 min. Note: this pose is very important and provides you with long term benefits. Try not to skip this. Close your eyes and imagine who you want to be and what your goals are! Always think happy thoughts.

Help the bunny to get from his home to the Wizard's hat!

WEEK 5

Did you know the Pacific Ocean is the largest ocean on Earth?

We have geographically divided our ocean into five regions: The Atlantic Ocean, The Pacific Ocean, The Indian Ocean, The Artic Ocean, and The Southern Ocean.

ARGOPREP

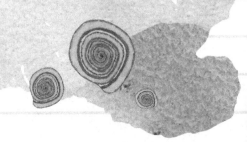

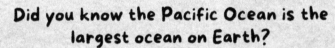

As you read and listen to people talk, it's important to understand exactly what they're expressing. One of the easiest ways people get tripped up is they misunderstand how sure something is. For example, there's a big difference between "Mikey might have the flu" and "Mikey has a serious case of the flu." Let's talk about words you can watch out for as you read and listen to ensure you're understanding how certain a situation is.

 Key Terms

Complete Certainty: Perfect knowledge that something is true, accurate, or factual

Strong Certainty: Knowledge that something is most likely to be true or fairly certain to happen

Partial Certainty: Belief or knowledge that something could reasonably happen

Uncertainty: Belief or hope that something might be true or may happen without any proof to back it up

For Example...

- Felicia will definitely do well on the test because she pays attention in class, she studied hard, and she has already gotten very high grades on all the previous tests.

  - This person is expressing complete certainty that Felicia will do well. The word "definitely" is an indicator. The author also provided several examples of good reasons why they were certain she would succeed.

- I assume Felicia will do well on the test because she is a strong student and always comes to class prepared.

  - This person is expressing strong certainty that Felicia will do well. The phrase "I assume Felicia will do well" shows that the author believes she is most likely going to succeed. Like the sentence that expressed complete certainty, this author provided examples.

- Felicia could do well on the test because she pays attention in class.
- Felicia might do well on the test because she pays attention in class.

  - These people are expressing partial certainty that Felicia will do well. The words "could" and "might" communicate that the person believes Felicia can do well, but they're not choosing words that show they have a large amount of belief or confidence in her.

- It's possible that Felicia will do well on the test.

  - This person is expressing uncertainty. They admit that Felicia doing well is one thing that could happen, but there's no confidence in the sentence that it probably will happen. Compared to the previous sentences, this one contains no examples or reasons why Felicia will do well, which demonstrates that the author doesn't believe it's a strong possibility.

The Salt Merchant and His Donkey
By Aesop

Back in ancient times, salt was considered extremely valuable - sometimes even more valuable than gold. That's why, one day, a merchant strapped some bags onto his donkey and went down to the seashore, hoping to get salt at a good price so he could increase his profits selling it to the people who lived inland. When he got to the seashore, the merchant filled his donkey's bags with salt, and he even bought more bags so the donkey could carry twice as much salt as he'd been originally planning.

On the walk home, the merchant and the donkey came to a place where they had to cross a stream. The merchant waded through just fine, but the donkey was so heavy with salt that it stumbled and dumped most of the valuable cargo into the water, where it was washed away. The merchant, extremely frustrated with the situation and the donkey, rode back to the seashore and bought even more salt than the first time.

When the merchant and the donkey returned to the same stream where the donkey had stumbled the first time, the donkey fell on purpose, spilling the extra salt so it was only carrying an amount that it was comfortable with. This time, the merchant realized what the donkey was doing, though, so he formed a new plan.

The merchant returned to the seashore again, but instead of salt, he bought huge bags full of sponges. He brought the donkey back to the stream, where it stumbled on purpose again to try and lighten its load. This time, however, the sponges in the donkey's bags became filled with water, making his load even heavier.

After that, the donkey never questioned how much salt his master gave him to carry.

1. How would you describe the donkey in this story?

2. How are the merchant's reactions to the donkey's first stumble and the donkey's second stumble different? Why?

3. Which key phrase helped you feel certain as a reader that the donkey's stumbling was not an accident?

   A. "Twice as much salt..." (Paragraph 1)
   B. "The donkey was so heavy with salt..." (Paragraph 2)
   C. "...on purpose..." (Paragraph 3)
   D. "...the amount that it was comfortable with..." (Paragraph 3)

4. Which of these statements can we be certain is true?

   A. The merchant in the story is always mean to his donkey.
   B. The donkey in the story is always lazy and disobedient.
   C. The merchant in the story is already fairly rich
   D. The donkey would've carried the salt if the merchant would've been nicer to him.

5. What is one other way the merchant could have solved his problem?

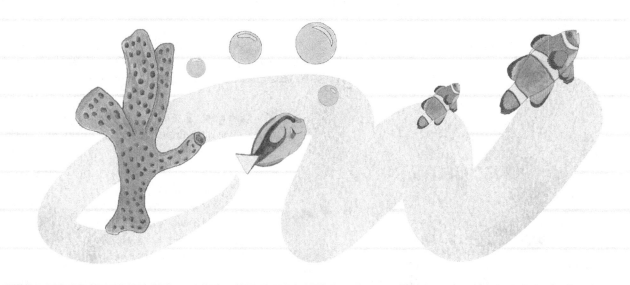

Comparing Degrees of Certainty

⭐ **Directions:**

Read each pair of sentences, then circle the sentence that expresses a **greater degree of certainty** and <u>underline the words</u> in both sentences that served as hints or helped you come up with your answer.

1. My older brother might be on the middle school soccer team this year because he is planning on trying out.

   My older sister is probably going to be on the middle school basketball team this year because she's the best shooter in her grade.

2. We're hoping to get rid of the mice in our house by getting a cat and setting some traps.

   We're calling an exterminator to help us with our mouse problem, so it should be over soon.

3. Ms. Fischer will definitely give us math homework tonight because we learned a new concept in class.

   It's highly likely we'll have to do jumping jacks in P.E. today because they're Mr. Lee's favorite.

4. I assume Monty has gone to the museum before because I know his parents and brother have been there.

   I think it's possible that I'll get invited to Jenna's birthday party.

5. There must be some important differences between alligators and crocodiles, or they wouldn't be considered two different animals.

   I believe one of the differences between alligators and crocodiles involves the shape of their snouts.

FITNESS

Please be aware of your environment and be safe at all times. If you cannot do an exercise, just try your best.

Repeat these **exercises 3 ROUNDS**

2 - Lunges: 2 times to each leg.
Note: Use your body weight or books as weight to do leg lunges.

4 - Run: 50m
Note: Run 25 meters to one side and 25 meters back to the starting position.

3 - Plank: 6 sec.

1 - Abs: 3 times

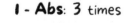

Two Great Painters
By James Baldwin

There was once a painter whose name was Zeuxis. He could paint pictures so life-like that they were mistaken for the real things which they represented.

At one time he painted the picture of some fruit which was so real that the birds flew down and pecked at it. This made him very proud of his skill.

"I am the only man in the world who can paint a picture so true to life," he said.

There was another famous artist whose name was Parrhasius. When he heard of the boast which Zeuxis had made, he said to himself, "I will see what I can do."

So he painted a beautiful picture which seemed to be covered with a curtain. Then he invited Zeuxis to come and see it.

Zeuxis looked at it closely. "Draw the curtain aside and show us the picture," he said.

Parrhasius laughed and answered, "The curtain is the picture."

"Well," said Zeuxis, "you have beaten me this time, and I shall boast no more. I deceived only the birds, but you have deceived me, a painter."

Some time after this, Zeuxis painted another wonderful picture. It was that of a boy carrying a basket of ripe red cherries. When he hung this painting outside of his door, some birds flew down and tried to carry the cherries away.

"Ah! this picture is a failure," he said. "For if the boy had been as well painted as the cherries, the birds would have been afraid to come near him."

1. How is the "certainty" of birds important to this story?

2. How are Zeuxis' and Parrhasius' personalities different from one another?

3. How confident is Zeuxis in his own abilities at the beginning of the story?

   A. Completely Certain
   B. Strong Certainty
   C. Partial Certainty
   D. Uncertain

4. How confident is Parrhasius in his ability to outdo Zeuxis at the beginning of the story?

   A. Complete Certainty
   B. Strong Certainty
   C. Partial Certainty
   D. Uncertain

5. How did Zeuxis' over-certainty in his talents actually lead to his confidence going down?

⭐ **Directions:**

Fill each blank with one of the words from the bank below to make the sentence express the degree of certainty listed in the parentheses after it.

MAYBE　　　　　DEFINITELY　　　　　PROBABLY

HOPEFULLY　　　　　COULD

1. Our dog Samantha will _____ live at least ten more years, but there's no way to be sure. (UNCERTAINTY)

2. _____ Grandma and Grandpa will come to our house for Thanksgiving Dinner because we went to their place last year. (PARTIAL CERTAINTY)

3. I _____ get a big hit in today's baseball game because I did great at practice this week. (PARTIAL CERTAINTY)

4. We will _____ go to the picnic because we've been looking forward to it all month. (STRONG CERTAINTY)

5. Green is _____ my favorite color of all time. (COMPLETE CERTAINTY)

FITNESS

Please be aware of your environment and be safe at all times. If you cannot do an exercise, just try your best.

Repeat these **exercises 3 ROUNDS**

1 - Squats: 5 times.
Note: imagine you are trying to sit on a chair.

2 - Side Bending: 5 times to each side. Note: try to touch your feet.

3 - Tree Pose: Stay as long as possible. Note: do the same with the other leg.

Tables/Charts and understanding data

The chart below shows how many yards Sam ran on some days. Answer questions 1 - 2, using the following data.

Day	Yards Ran
Monday	732
Tuesday	540
Wednesday	658
Thursday	830

1. Which day did Sam run the fewest yards?

   A. Monday
   B. Tuesday
   C. Wednesday
   D. Thursday

2. How many yards did Sam run on Wednesday and Thursday in total?

   A. 1,272
   B. 1,198
   C. 1,370
   D. 1,488

Jules looked in the fridge and found some tomatoes, onions, and lemons. She made a chart to log the food she found.

Food			
How many?	18	10	6

Answer questions 3 - 4, using the data above.

3. Out of the three items in the fridge, which item was the lowest in quantity?

   A. Tomatoes
   B. Onions
   C. Lemons
   D. They are all equal

4. How many more tomatoes were there than lemons?

   A. 12
   B. 8
   C. 6
   D. 4

Bar graph & Line graph

Use the following bar graph to answer questions 1 - 2.

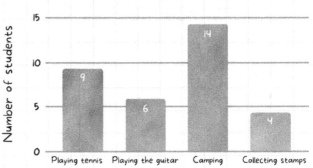

1. How many students were surveyed in total?

   A. 26
   B. 29
   C. 31
   D. 33

2. Which hobby is the most popular?

   Answer _____

Some friends found seashells on the beach and recorded their quantity. Using the data from the bar graph, answer questions 3 - 4.

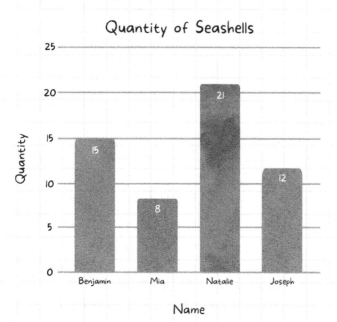

Quantity of Seashells

3. Which friend found the most seashells?

   A. Benjamin
   B. Mia
   C. Natalie
   D. Joseph

4. How many more seashells did Natalie find than Mia?

   A. 15
   B. 13
   C. 8
   D. 7

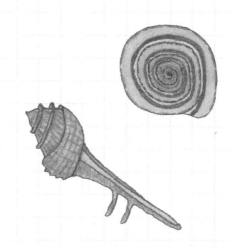

FITNESS

Repeat these exercises 3 ROUNDS

Please be aware of your environment and be safe at all times. If you cannot do an exercise, just try your best.

1 - Bend forward: 10 times.
Note: try to touch your feet. Make sure to keep your back straight and if needed you can bend your knees.

2 - Lunges: 3 times to each leg.
Note: Use your body weight or books as weight to do leg lunges.

3 - Plank: 6 sec.

4 - Abs: 10 times

97

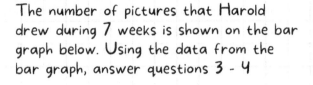

Bar graph & Line graph

Stacy graphed the yards she walked during **6** days. Using the data from the bar graph, answer questions 1 - 2.

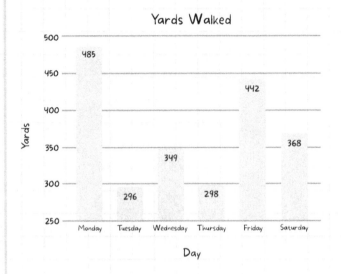

Yards Walked

The number of pictures that Harold drew during **7** weeks is shown on the bar graph below. Using the data from the bar graph, answer questions 3 - 4

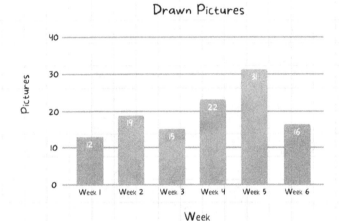

Drawn Pictures

1. How many yards did Stacy walk on Monday, Thursday and Saturday in total?

   A. 1,151
   B. 1,132
   C. 1,234
   D. 986

2. How many more yards did she walk on Friday than on Tuesday?

   A. 137
   B. 126
   C. 146
   D. 158

3. How many more pictures did Harold draw on week **5** than week **4**?

   A. 6
   B. 8
   C. 9
   D. 10

4. How many pictures were drawn on weeks 1, 2, 3 and 6 in all?

   A. 56
   B. 62
   C. 67
   D. 58

The bar graph below shows the number of basketball courts in each park. Use the following bar graph to answer questions 5 - 6.

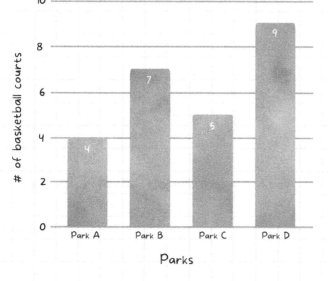

# of basketball courts in parks

# of basketball courts

10
8
6
4
2
0

Park A (4) Park B (7) Park C (5) Park D (9)

Parks

5. Which park has the most basketball courts?

A. Park A
B. Park B
C. Park C
D. Park D

6. How many more basketball courts are at Parks C and D than at Parks A and B?

Answer _____

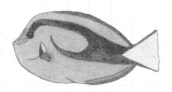

FITNESS

Repeat these **exercises 3 ROUNDS**

Please be aware of your environment and be safe at all times. If you cannot do an exercise, just try your best.

1 - High Plank: 6 sec.

2 - Chair: 10 sec. Note: sit on an imaginary chair, keep your back straight.

3 - Waist Hooping: 10 times. Note: if you do not have a hoop, pretend you have an imaginary hoop and rotate your hips 10 times.

4 - Abs: 10 times

Line of symmetry

1. How many lines of symmetry does this shape have?

   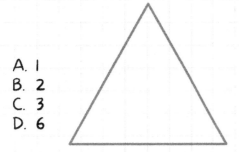

   A. 1
   B. 2
   C. 3
   D. 6

2. Which shape appears to have EXACTLY 1 line of symmetry?

   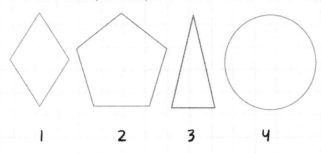

   1   2   3   4

   A. 1
   B. 2
   C. 3
   D. 4

3. Draw all the lines of symmetry for this shape.

4. In the shape below, which of the following is a line of symmetry?

   A. AB
   B. CD
   C. EF
   D. YZ

   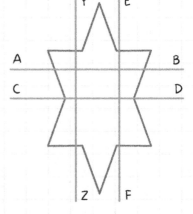

5. Is this shape symmetrical? How do you know?

   Answer _____

6. Which object appears to have more than 1 line of symmetry?

   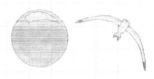

   1   2   3   4

   A. 1
   B. 2
   C. 3
   D. 4

7. Draw all the lines of symmetry for this object.

8. How many lines of symmetry does this object have?

A. 1
B. 4
C. 8
D. 16

9. Which object has EXACTLY 4 lines of symmetry?

1   2   3   4

A. 1
B. 2
C. 3
D. 4

10. How many lines of symmetry does this shape have?

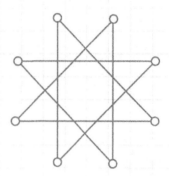

Answer _____

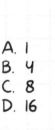

YOGA

Please be aware of your environment and be safe at all times. If you cannot do an exercise, just try your best.

1 - Down Dog: 10 sec.

2 - Bend Down: 10 sec.

3 - Chair: 10 sec.

4 - Child Pose: 20 sec.

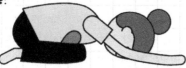

5 - Shavasana: as long as you can. Note: think of happy moments and relax your mind.

WEEK 5 DAY 6 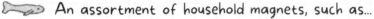 EXPERIMENT

Comparing Magnetic Force

When we made our racetrack, we said **force** was a push or a pull that impacts an object's **motion**. One kind of **force** we can observe in everyday life is magnetism. Magnets have a **charge** that might attract, repel, or have no affect at all on objects, depending on what those objects are made from.

Materials:

- An assortment of household magnets, such as...
  - Refrigerator magnets
  - Disc magnets
  - Bar magnets
  - Any handheld tools with magnets on them (flashlights, screwdrivers, etc.)
- A variety of small metal objects, such as...
  - Staples
  - Paper clips
  - Coins
  - Scissors
  - Keys
  - Screws or nails
- Note paper

Procedure:

1. Begin by separating out the different kinds of magnets you have and briefly describe each one on your note paper. Describe what the magnet **looks like**, what it **feels like**, and how **big it is**. After you've looked at all the magnets, make some predictions about which ones you think will be the **best or strongest** and why.

2. Arrange your small metal objects on a tabletop, and **slowly move the magnet near and around each one**. On your note sheet, keep track of which objects the magnet can **pick up**, which objects the magnet can **stick to**, and which objects the magnet **seemingly has no effect on**. As you go, think about which magnets are working the best and which ones are the weakest.

3. Once you've tested all your magnets, clear the table and set all the small metal objects aside.

4. Next, test to **see how your different magnets interact with each other**. (**NOTE**: Be careful as you do this, as some magnets might want to stick together or force each other apart stronger than you are expecting!) Take two different magnets and bring them close to each other, rotating them to see how all sides interact with each other. Observe whether they seem to want to stick together, force apart, or have no interaction at all, and **write the results on your note paper**. Repeat this process until you've compared all the magnets.

5. Answer the questions below and **gather up your materials**. You'll want to use these same magnets and metal objects for next week's experiment.

Follow-Up Questions:

1. What did you learn about some of the different kinds of magnets you have around your house? Which ones were **able to do things the other magnets couldn't?**

~~~~~~

~~~~~~

~~~~~~

2. Did you have any metal objects that the magnets couldn't pick up? Which ones were they?

~~~~~~

~~~~~~

~~~~~~

YOGA

Please be aware of your environment and be safe at all times. If you cannot do an exercise, just try your best.

1 - Tree Pose: Stay as long as possible. Note: do on one leg then on another.

2 - Down Dog: 10 sec.

3 - Stretching: Stay as long as possible. Note: do on one leg then on another.

6 - Shavasana: 5 min. Note: this pose is very important and provides you with long term benefits. Try not to skip this. Close your eyes and imagine who you want to be and what your goals are! Always think happy thoughts.

5 - Book Pose: 6 sec. Note: Keep your core tight. Legs should be across from your eyes.

4 - Lower Plank: 6 sec. Note: Keep your back straight and body tight.

Task: Help Amy the astronaut find the correct way to the rocket. Color in the pathway so Amy the astronaut can take off!

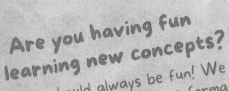

Are you having fun learning new concepts? Learning should always be fun! We tend to remember more information when we enjoy the learning experience.

WEEK 6

It's a goldfish!
You have probably seen this creature since the goldfish is the most popular aquarium fish. Here's a fun fact: A goldfish can see more colors than a human!

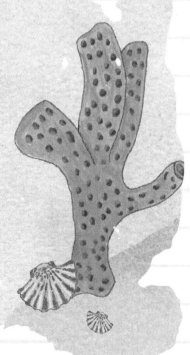

ARGOPREP

As you begin to read more advanced texts, you'll find that people sometimes use words to represent something other than their basic meaning. We call that **figurative language**. Identifying figurative language in texts you read, while also introducing it to your own writing shows that you are a master of language!

Key Terms

Literal Meaning: The most basic level of language, where the focus is on being clear and communicating basic meaning

Figurative Language: Using comparisons, analogies, or other tricks of language to make writing more descriptive and less literal

Basic Forms of Figurative Language:

Type of Fig. Language	Definition	Example
Simile	A comparison between two things that uses either the word **like** or **as**.	Ms. Hutchins is wise **like** an owl. OR She is **as** fast **as** a cheetah on the basketball court.
Metaphor	A comparison between two things that does <u>not</u> use like or as.	Ms. Hutchins **is** a wise old owl. OR She **is** a sprinting cheetah on the basketball court.
Personification	Describing an object or animal as though it has human qualities.	The wind **pulled** at my hair and **whispered** into my ear with its cold **breath**.
Hyperbole	Exaggerating or over-stating something to make a point.	Our air conditioning is broken, so it is **like a thousand degrees** in our house.

Focusing on literal meaning is really important to make sure you're choosing words that communicate ideas clearly. However, figurative language provides you more opportunities to be creative.

For Example...

- Jennifer is a very tall person.

Can become...

- Jennifer is **as tall as her mom's car** when she stands next to it. (SIMILE)
- Jennifer **is a giraffe** living in a world of ants. (METAPHOR)
- Jennifer is so tall that **lamp posts get jealous** of her. (PERSONIFICATION)
- When you first meet her, it's easy to think Jennifer is **at least eight feet tall**. (HYPERBOLE)

The Thief and the Innkeeper
By Aesop

A thief checked into a hotel room that he knew he couldn't pay for, but he planned to steal something valuable to pay for the room before the time he checked out. After a few days at the inn, the thief was worried because he hadn't found anything worth enough money to pay for his room. He began to notice that the innkeeper had a very nice new coat, though, and he thought that if he could get ahold of that, he might be able to cover the bill.

The thief sat down with the innkeeper and started a long, rambling conversation about all sorts of different topics. After he'd talked the innkeeper's ear off for several hours, the thief started making big yawning noises. As he yawned, he would occasionally also howl like a wolf. After a few minutes of this, the innkeeper was very disturbed.

"Why are you howling like a wolf?" he asked.

"I will tell you," the thief said, "but first hold onto my clothes. When I get these yawning attacks, I turn into a wolf and attack people. The worst part is that my clothes get completely torn up and ruined every time."

The innkeeper was very nervous as the thief handed him his jacket and socks, but it only got worse when the thief began yawning and howling again.

"Please, take my clothes!" the thief begged. "I'm about to turn into a wolf!"

The innkeeper screamed in fear and ran out of the room. Not only did he leave the thief's clothes behind, he also forgot to grab his beautiful new coat, which the thief snatched as he walked out the door.

The moral of the story: Not every tale should be believed.

1. What is the thief's original plan when he checks into the hotel room?

~~~~~~

~~~~~~

2. How is what happens at the end of the story different from the thief's original plan?

~~~~~~

~~~~~~

~~~~~~

3. What kind of figurative language is used in the phrase "...howl like a wolf?"

A. Simile
B. Metaphor
C. Personification
D. Hyperbole

4. Which of these phrases from the passage contains **figurative language**?

A. "He planned to steal something valuable to pay for the room..."
B. "The thief started making big yawning noises..."
C. "After he'd talked the innkeeper's ear off for several hours..."
D. "It only got worse when the thief began yawning and howling again..."

5. How could the thief have approached this situation in an honest way? Give one or two examples:

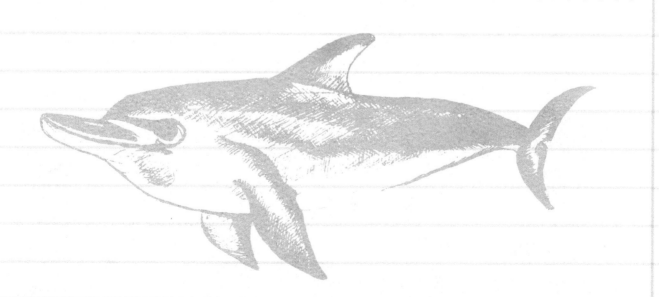

Identifying Basic Forms of Figurative Language

⭐ **Directions:**

Underline the example of figurative language in each sentence and then write whether it is an example of a **simile, metaphor, personification, or hyperbole.**

1. I was hoping to go for a run outside, but of course it turned out to be the crummiest day of the whole year.

2. Our dog is a monster when it comes to food.

3. My smartphone is my best friend because it helps me get the information I need, and I can play games on it.

4. The sun was so hot I felt like an egg frying in a pan.

5. Mrs. Turner is the strictest principal in the history of school.

FITNESS

Please be aware of your environment and be safe at all times. If you cannot do an exercise, just try your best.

2 - Lunges: 2 times to each leg.
Note: Use your body weight or books as weight to do leg lunges.

Repeat these **exercises 3 ROUNDS**

4 - Run: 50m
Note: Run 25 meters to one side and 25 meters back to the starting position.

3 - Plank: 6 sec.

1 - Abs: 3 times

The Surly Guest
By James Baldwin

One day John Randolph, of Roanoke, set out on horseback to ride to a town that was many miles from his home. The road was strange to him, and he traveled very slowly.

When night came on he stopped at a pleasant roadside inn and asked for lodging. The innkeeper welcomed him kindly. He had often heard of the great John Randolph, and therefore he did all that he could to entertain him well.

A fine supper was prepared, and the innkeeper himself waited upon his guest. John Randolph ate in silence. The innkeeper spoke of the weather, of the roads, of the crops, of politics. But his surly guest said scarcely a word.

In the morning a good breakfast was served, and then Mr. Randolph made ready to start on his journey. He called for his bill and paid it. His horse was led to the door, and a servant helped him to mount it.

As he was starting away, the friendly innkeeper said, "Which way will you travel, Mr. Randolph?"

Mr. Randolph looked at him in no gentle way, and answered, "Sir!"

"I only asked which way you intend to travel," said the man.

"Oh! Have I paid you my bill?"

"Yes, sir."

"Do I owe you anything more?"

"No, sir."

"Then, I intend to travel the way I wish to go, do you understand?"

He turned his horse and rode away. He had not gone farther than to the end of the innkeeper's field, when to his surprise he found that the road forked. He did not know whether he should take the right-hand fork or the left-hand.

He paused for a while. There was no signboard to help him. He looked back and saw the innkeeper still standing by the door. He called to him: "My friend, which of these roads shall I travel to go to Lynchburg?"

"Mr. Randolph," answered the innkeeper, "you have paid your bill and don't owe me a cent. Travel the way you wish to go. Good-bye!"

As bad luck would have it, Mr. Randolph took the wrong road. He went far out of his way and lost much time, all on account of his surliness.

1. Based on the passage, what are some other words that mean the same thing (or close to the same thing) as surly?

2. How is the **figurative meaning** of Mr. Randolph's question "Do I owe you anything more?" different from the **literal meaning** of his words?

3. Which description early in the story is later proven to be false or incorrect?

   A. "...a pleasant roadside inn..."
   B. "...welcomed him kindly..."
   C. "...the great John Randolph..."
   D. "...a fine supper..."

4. Which of these phrases from the passage contains **figurative language**?

   A. "The innkeeper spoke of the weather..."
   B. "...he found out that the road forked."
   C. "There was no signboard to help him..."
   D. "He went far out of his way and lost much time..."

5. Create **three** similes or metaphors that could describe **John Randolph**. Then, create **three** similes or metaphors that could describe the **Innkeeper**.

John Randolph:

Innkeeper:

⭐ **Directions:**

Complete the sentences by adding your own examples of figurative language as described in the parentheses.

1. Trevor is _____ when he runs.

   (Create a SIMILE about how FAST Trevor is)

2. My cousin Francine is _____

   _____ .

   (Create a METAPHOR about how SMART Francine is)

3. The first time I ever saw a horror movie, I thought I was going to _____

   _____ .

   (Use HYPERBOLE to describe how SCARED you were by the movie)

4. The bicycle _____

   _____ which made the rider fall.

   (Use PERSONIFICATION to describe how the BICYCLE made the rider fall)

5. I created a painting that was _____

   _____ in art class last week.

   (Create a SIMILE about how COLORFUL the painting is)

FITNESS

Please be aware of your environment and be safe at all times. If you cannot do an exercise, just try your best.

Repeat these **exercises 3 ROUNDS**

1 - Squats: 5 times.
Note: imagine you are trying to sit on a chair.

2 - Side Bending: 5 times to each side. Note: try to touch your feet.

3 - Tree Pose: Stay as long as possible. Note: do the same with the other leg.

Identifying perpendicular lines, parallel lines, points, lines and rays.

Use the drawing below to answer questions 1 - 2.

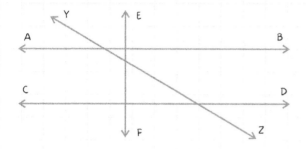

1. Which lines are parallel?

   A. AB and CD
   B. AB and EF
   C. EF and YZ
   D. CD and YZ

2. Which lines are perpendicular?

   A. AB and CD
   B. AB and EF
   C. EF and YZ
   D. CD and YZ

Use the drawing below to answer questions 3 - 4.

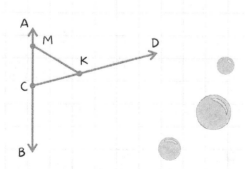

3. Which of the following answer choices is a line?

   A. AB
   B. CD
   C. MK
   D. CK

4. Which of the following answer choices is a ray?

   A. AB
   B. CD
   C. MK
   D. CK

Use the drawing below to answer questions 5 - 6.

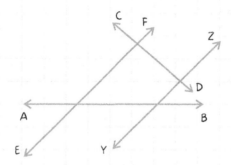

5. Which lines are perpendicular?

   A. AB and CD
   B. AB and EF
   C. EF and YZ
   D. CD and YZ

6. Which lines are parallel?

   A. AB and CD
   B. AB and EF
   C. EF and YZ
   D. CD and YZ

Use the drawing below to answer questions 7 - 8.

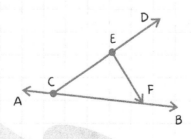

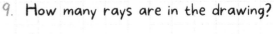

7. What is CD?

    A. A line
    B. A line segment
    C. A ray
    D. A point

8. What is E?

    A. A line
    B. A line segment
    C. A ray
    D. A point

9. How many rays are in the drawing?

    A. 1
    B. 2
    C. 3
    D. 4

10. How many lines are in the drawing?

    A. 1
    B. 2
    C. 3
    D. 4

Use the drawing below to answer questions 9 - 10.

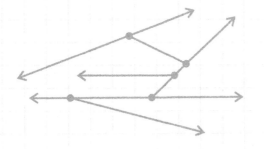

FITNESS

Repeat these **exercises 3 ROUNDS**

Please be aware of your environment and be safe at all times. If you cannot do an exercise, just try your best.

1 - Bend forward: 10 times.
Note: try to touch your feet. Make sure to keep your back straight and if needed you can bend your knees.

2 - Lunges: 3 times to each leg.
Note: Use your body weight or books as weight to do leg lunges.

4 - Abs: 10 times

3 - Plank: 6 sec.

WEEK 6 DAY 4 MATH

Time

1. What time is represented on the clock below?

   A. Thirty-seven five
   B. Five forty
   C. Forty four
   D. Four thirty-eight

2. What time does the clock show?

   A. 1:53
   B. 12:43
   C. 12:53
   D. 1:50

3. What time will it be in one hour and twenty-five minutes?

   A. 3:55
   B. 4:30
   C. 4:35
   D. 4:25

4. Look at the digital clock:

   ```
   9:35
   ```

   Which analog clock shows the same time?

   | 1 | 2 | 3 | 4 |

   A. 1
   B. 2
   C. 3
   D. 4

5. Mrs. Clark is cooking breakfast. The clock shows:

   What time is it?

   A. 6:23 am
   B. 7:23 am
   C. 6:23 pm
   D. 7:23 pm

6. What is the elapsed time between the two times represented on the clocks below?

      `7:05`

   Answer _____

7. Trish is going to the gym in 2 and a half hours. It is now 2:45 pm. What time is Trish going to the gym?

   Answer _____

8. Jim is eating soup for lunch. The clock shows:

   What time is it?

   A. 2:50 am
   B. 3:50 am
   C. 2:50 pm
   D. 3:50 pm

9. What is another way to write 1:12 pm in words?

   Answer _____

10. What is the elapsed time between 10:55 am and 2:18 pm?

Answer _____

Unit conversions (minutes, seconds, hours, liters, etc)

1. How many seconds are in 7 minutes?

   A. 360 seconds
   B. 380 seconds
   C. 420 seconds
   D. 480 seconds

2. Which of the following completes the equation?

   5,700 grams = ____ kilograms + ____ grams

   Answer _____

3. If a bag of sugar weighs about 3 kilograms, how many grams does the bag of sugar weigh?

   A. 30 grams
   B. 30,000 grams
   C. 3,000 grams
   D. 300 grams

4. Which symbol makes the following inequality TRUE?

   7 liters _____ 560 ml.

   A. >
   B. <
   C. =
   D. +

5. How many minutes are in 4 hours?

   A. 180 minutes
   B. 120 minutes
   C. 220 minutes
   D. 240 minutes

6. How many milliliters are in 8 liters?

   A. 8,000 mL
   B. 800 mL
   C. 80 mL
   D. 8 mL

7. Convert: 48 hours = ____ days.

   Answer _____

8. Find 136 cm subtracted from 3 m.

   Answer _____

FITNESS

Please be aware of your environment and be safe at all times. If you cannot do an exercise, just try your best.

Repeat these exercises **3 ROUNDS**

1 - High Plank: 6 sec.

2 - Chair: 10 sec. Note: sit on an imaginary chair, keep your back straight.

3 - Waist Hooping: 10 times. Note: if you do not have a hoop, pretend you have an imaginary hoop and rotate your hips 10 times.

4 - Abs: 10 times

Word problems for unit conversions

1. Hannah has **3** containers that each have **3** liters of water in them. How many milliliters of water does Hannah have in total?

   A. **9** mL
   B. **90** mL
   C. **900** mL
   D. **9,000** mL

2. Mike has five bags of potatoes that each weigh **6,000** grams. How many kilograms of potatoes does he have?

   A. **3** kilograms
   B. **30** kilograms
   C. **300** kilograms
   D. **3,000** kilograms

3. Roger spends **17** minutes to get to his school. How many seconds does it take for him to get to school?

   A. **960** seconds
   B. **980** seconds
   C. **1,020** seconds
   D. **1,080** seconds

4. Haley finished studying for her math exam at **5** pm. If her study time was **75** minutes long, what time did she start to study?

   A. **3:45** pm
   B. **3:55** pm
   C. **3:35** pm
   D. **2:55** pm

5. Teddy bought **1,300** grams of flour. How much flour did Teddy buy in kilograms?

   A. **1** kilogram and **100** grams
   B. **1** kilogram and **500** grams
   C. **1** kilogram and **300** grams
   D. **1** kilogram and **600** grams

6. Lilly has five cartons of juice that each contains **800** mL in them. How many liters do the five cartons hold altogether?

   Answer _____

7. Molly weighed her cat. The cat weighed **4** kilograms and **500** grams. Convert this measurement into grams.

   Answer _____

8. Willy's basketball weighs **2,000** grams. What is its weight in kilograms?

   Answer _____

9. There are **9,000** milliliters of apple juice in a container. How many liters are there in all?

   Answer _____

10. Jeffrey enjoys reading magazines. . It was **5:39** pm when he started reading. It took him **86** minutes to read it till the end. What time was it when Jeffrey finished reading the magazine?

    Answer _____

Word problems dealing with mass and volume

1. If three buckets below are equal, how much does the second bucket hold?

8 liters   ?   ?

A. 80 milliliters
B. 800 milliliters
C. 8 milliliter
D. 8,000 milliliters

2. How many in total can the three buckets above hold?

Answer _____

YOGA

3. There was an aquarium that held 15 liters of water. The cup can hold $\frac{1}{2}$ liter.

How many cups do you need to fill the aquarium?

A. 15 cups
B. 20 cups
C. 30 cups
D. 35 cups

4. There are 100 grams of vitamins per bottle. How many grams of vitamins are there in 11 bottles?

Answer _____

5. If one book has a mass of 7 grams, then what is the mass of 17 books?

A. 109 g
B. 119 g
C. 129 g
D. 139 g

Please be aware of your environment and be safe at all times. If you cannot do an exercise, just try your best.

1 - Down Dog: 10 sec.

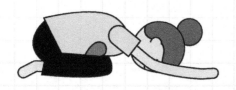

2 - Bend Down: 10 sec.

3 - Chair: 10 sec.

4 - Child Pose: 20 sec.

5 - Shavasana: as long as you can. Note: think of happy moments and relax your mind.

WEEK 6 DAY 6 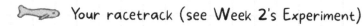 EXPERIMENT

Using Magnetic Force to Move Objects

Now that we've seen magnetism at work, let's think about how we can use magnets and magnetic force to **create motion**.

Materials:

- Your racetrack (see Week 2's Experiment)
- An assortment of household magnets, such as...
  - Refrigerator magnets
  - Disc magnets
  - Bar magnets
  - Any handheld tools with magnets on them (flashlights, screwdrivers, etc.)
- A variety of small metal objects, such as...
  - Staples
  - Paper clips
  - Coins
  - Scissors
  - Keys
  - Screws or nails
- Note paper

Procedure:

1. Set up your racetrack, but instead of propping it up like a ramp, **lay it flat** on a tabletop or floor.

2. Gather your small metal objects. It's ideal if they're the same ones you used last week, but they don't have to be. **NOTE:** If you want, you can use your balance to compare the masses of the objects before you go any further. If you do that, be sure to rank them on your notepaper!

3. Place one of your metal objects at one end of the track. Then, take your **weakest magnet** (based on your notes from last week) and, holding the magnet above the track, see if you can move the metal object down the track by sliding the magnet above it. If you can't move the object at all (or can only pick it up with the magnet without getting the object to move down the track) try a different magnet.

4. **Test all your different metal objects using all your different magnets** and make note of which magnets can effectively move the object down the track, and which objects are the easiest for the magnets to move.

5. Answer the questions below, and then put your materials away. **We are officially done with the racetrack for the summer,** but you can keep it for your own future experiments, if you want!

121

Follow-Up Questions:

1. How did this experience show you that the **strongest magnet isn't always the best** tool for every job?

2. Which magnet/metal object pairing did you find was the **easiest to move effectively** down the track? **Why** do you think that combination worked so well?

YOGA

Please be aware of your environment and be safe at all times. If you cannot do an exercise, just try your best.

3 - Stretching: Stay as long as possible. Note: do on one leg then on another.

1 - Tree Pose: Stay as long as possible. Note: do on one leg then on another.

2 - Down Dog: 10 sec.

5 - Book Pose: 6 sec. Note: Keep your core tight. Legs should be across from your eyes.

6 - Shavasana: 5 min. Note: this pose is very important and provides you with long term benefits. Try not to skip this. Close your eyes and imagine who you want to be and what your goals are! Always think happy thoughts.

4 - Lower Plank: 6 sec. Note: Keep your back straight and body tight.

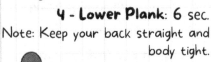
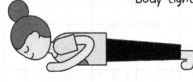

Task: Meet Giraffe 1, 2, 3, 4 and 5! Help the giraffes match their number with the correct letter (body).

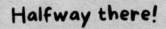

Halfway there!

You have successfully completed half of this workbook. Are you excited to continue learning? I sure am.

WEEK 7

It's a turtle!

Turtles are reptiles that can live over 100 years. Sea turtles in particular have been known to have a lifespan over 150+ years.

ARGOPREP

One crucial skill you need as a reader is the ability to recognize whether what you're reading is **fact** or **opinion.** While this sounds simple at first, it can actually be very tricky because people tend to be very confident in their opinions and present them as though they are facts. However, a little thinking and a little research can quickly help you tell whether what you're reading is indisputably true or just an opinion.

 Key Terms

Fact: Something that can be proven as definitely true

Opinion: Something that someone thinks, believes, or hopes is true

When people state their opinion, there are usually words or phrases that serve as **hints** that someone is sharing their **personal perspective,** rather than stating something that is undeniably true. Here are a few of those "watch words" to look out for. If you see any of these, you're reading a statement of **opinion, not fact!**

Words & Phrases that Clearly Indicate Opinion		
I think	I feel	I hope
I believe	In my opinion	From my point of view
It seems to me	I am confident that	My perspective

People don't always use phrases like these, though. In fact, sometimes, people just **present their opinions as though they are facts** to show their confidence and try to convince people to see things their way.

That means that in order to be sure something is **actually a fact**, you need to:

● **Look for evidence**, support, or examples in the sentence that show that something is definitely true

● Ask yourself, "**Could someone disagree with this statement** without necessarily being wrong?"

  ● If you can disagree with something without being wrong, that proves it is a fact and not an opinion.

For Example...

In the sentence...

🌀 I believe Mark is the best choice for class president. **(OPINION)**

🐚 The phrase "I believe..." at the beginning tips us off that this is an opinion.

🌀 Mark is the best choice for class president. **(OPINION PRESENTED AS FACT)**

🐚 The speaker here never says "I believe," **but** they don't offer any specific evidence to back up their point, and someone could easily disagree with this statement and **not necessarily be wrong**.

🌀 Mark is a strong candidate for class president because he is a good student and he communicates very well with his classmates. **(FACT)**

🐚 The speaker avoids being too dramatic about how good a candidate Mark is (they avoid saying he is "the best") and also provides specific pieces of evidence to back up their point of view.

The Apes and the Two Travelers
By Aesop

Two men, one who always spoke the truth and the other who told nothing but lies, were traveling together and by chance came to the land of Apes. One of the Apes, who had raised himself to be king, commanded them to be seized and brought before him, that he might know what was said of him among men.

He ordered at the same time that all the Apes be arranged in a long row on his right hand and on his left, and that a throne be placed for him, as was the custom among men. After these preparations he signified that the two men should be brought before him, and greeted them with this salutation: "What sort of a king do I seem to you to be, O strangers?"

The Lying Traveler replied, "You seem to me a most mighty king."

"And what is your estimate of those you see around me?"

"These," he made answer, "are worthy companions of yourself, fit at least to be ambassadors and leaders of armies."

The Ape and all his court, gratified with the lie, commanded that a handsome present be given to the flatterer. On this the truthful Traveler thought to himself, "If so great a reward be given for a lie, with what gift may not I be rewarded, if, according to my custom, I tell the truth?"

The Ape quickly turned to him. "And pray how do I and these my friends around me seem to you?"

"Thou art," he said, "a most excellent Ape, and all these thy companions after thy example are excellent Apes too." The King of the Apes, enraged at hearing these truths, gave him over to the teeth and claws of his companions.

1. How would you describe the King of the Apes in the story?

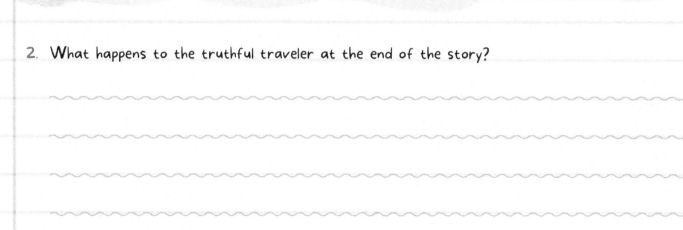
2. What happens to the truthful traveler at the end of the story?

3. Which of these statements about the story is a **fact**?

   A. The lying traveler should not have been rewarded
   B. The truthful traveler should not have been punished
   C. The King of the Apes wanted to be flattered
   D. The truthful traveler should have chosen better words

4. Which of these statements about the story is an **opinion**?

   A. The truthful traveler should have lied
   B. The Ape King was quick to punish the truthful traveler
   C. The lying traveler saved his own life by refusing to tell the truth
   D. The lying traveler got a present from the Ape King

5. Based on the story, why can it be harder or more frustrating to focus on **facts**, rather than just sharing an **opinion**?

⭐ **Directions:**

Read each sentence, then write on the line below whether it is **fact** or **opinion**. Once you've done that, circle the words in the sentence that helped you choose your answer.

1. The Boston Red Sox are the best team in the whole world.

   _____

2. I know I am sick because I took my temperature and I have a fever of 101 degrees.

   _____

3. Ms. Foster is mean because she always gives me lunch detention when I forget my homework.

   _____

4. Tiger Woods is one of the most important golfers of all time because he has won more than 105 professional tournaments and has helped the game grow in popularity.

   _____

5. Everybody loves Thanksgiving because it is the time of year when families come together to celebrate what they are thankful for, eat a delicious meal, and watch football.

   _____

 **FITNESS**

Please be aware of your environment and be safe at all times. If you cannot do an exercise, just try your best.

Repeat these **exercises 3 ROUNDS**

2 - Lunges: 2 times to each leg.
Note: Use your body weight or books as weight to do leg lunges.

4 - Run: 50m
Note: Run 25 meters to one side and 25 meters back to the starting position.

1 - Abs: 3 times

3 - Plank: 6 sec.

The Dark Day
By James Baldwin

Listen, and I will tell you of the famous dark day in Connecticut. It was in the month of May, more than a hundred years ago.

The sun rose bright and fair, and the morning was without a cloud. The air was very still. There was not a breath of wind to stir the young leaves on the trees.

Then, about the middle of the day, it began to grow dark. The sun was hidden. A black cloud seemed to cover the earth.

The birds flew to their nests. The chickens went to roost. The cows came home from the pasture and stood mooing at the gate. It grew so dark that the people could not see their way along the streets.

Then everybody began to feel frightened. "What is the matter? What is going to happen?" each one asked of another. The children cried. The dogs howled. The women wept, and some of the men prayed.

"The end of the world has come!" cried some; and they ran about in the darkness.

"This is the last great day!" cried others; and they knelt down and waited.

In the old statehouse, the wise men of Connecticut were sitting. They were men who made the laws, and much depended upon their wisdom.

When the darkness came, they too began to be alarmed. The gloom was terrible.

"It is the day of the Lord." said one.

"No use to make laws," said another, "for they will never be needed."

"I move that we adjourn," said a third.

Then up from his seat rose Abraham Davenport.

His voice was clear and strong, and all knew that he, at least, was not afraid.

"This may be the last great day," he said. "I do not know whether the end of the world has come or not. But I am sure that it is my duty to stand at my post as long as I live. So, let us go on with the work that is before us. Let the candles be lighted."

His words put courage into every heart. The candles were brought in. Then with his strong face aglow in their feeble light, he made a speech in favor of a law to help poor fishermen.

And as he spoke, the other lawmakers listened in silence till the darkness began to fade and the sky grew bright again.

1. Based on this story, how would you describe Abraham Davenport's personality?

2. How are the other people at the statehouse different from Abraham Davenport?

3. Which of these lines from the passage shows a character expressing an opinion?
   A. "What is the matter?"
   B. "This is the last great day!"
   C. "I do not know whether the end of the world has come or not..."
   D. "When the darkness came, they began to be alarmed."

4. Why does Abraham Davenport propose the law to help poor fisherman?
   A. To show that people should continue living as normal, even though confusing things were happening outside
   B. To show people that even very poor people are important to a successful society
   C. To show people he wasn't scared of the dark
   D. To show people that the same things are important in the darkness that are important in the light

5. How does this story show that opinion can get out of control when people don't have enough facts?

 Directions:

Read each sentence, then write on the line below whether it is **fact** or **opinion**. Once you've done that, circle the words in the sentence that helped you choose your answer.

1. Nobody likes video games with bad graphics because they are boring to look at.

2. Christine knits the most beautiful scarves I've seen in my life.

3. Clean drinking water is crucial to public health because our bodies need hydration and contaminants in water can be extremely dangerous.

4. World War II occurred between 1939 and 1945, with battles taking place in both Europe and the Pacific.

5. My dad's car is much cooler than my mom's because it's a red sports car.

FITNESS

Please be aware of your environment and be safe at all times. If you cannot do an exercise, just try your best.

Repeat these **exercises 3 ROUNDS**

2 - Side Bending: 5 times to each side. Note: try to touch your feet.

1 - Squats: 5 times. Note: imagine you are trying to sit on a chair.

3 - Tree Pose: Stay as long as possible. Note: do the same with the other leg.

Word problems dealing with mass and volume

1. Franny bought 3 pounds of sweets. James bought 51 ounces of sweets. Who bought more sweets? Prove your answer.

   A. Franny bought more because she bought pounds and pounds is greater than ounces.

   B. They bought the same amount because 3 pounds = 51 ounces.

   C. James bought more because 3 pounds is 48 ounces and James bought 51 ounces of sweets.

   D. James bought more because 51 > 3.

2. A coffee machine can store 8 liters of coffee. How much coffee can it store in mL?

   A. 8 mL
   B. 80 mL
   C. 800 mL
   D. 8,000 mL

3. The weight of 4 cats is shown below.

Cats	Pounds
1	9
2	6
3	15
4	10

   If all 4 cats were placed on a scale, how much would the scale read, in ounces?

   A. 640 oz
   B. 320 oz
   C. 76 oz
   D. 1,820 oz

4. Alexander caught 3 fishes that were 2 kg and 200 g, 2 kg and 400 g, 3 kg and 150 g in weight. How many kilograms did the three fishes weigh together?

   Answer _____

5. A farmer wanted to determine the weight of a hen. Which of the following is the best estimate for the weight of a hen?

   A. 3 kilograms
   B. 100 grams
   C. 30 centimeters
   D. 30 decimeters

Temperature (Celcius) °

1. What is the temperature?

   A. 0°
   B. 5°
   C. 10°
   D. 15°

2. On Monday morning the temperature was 23° Celsius. At the night time the temperature dropped 9° Celsius. What was the temperature at the night time?

   A. 9° C
   B. 12° C
   C. 14° C
   D. 32° C

3. What is the difference between the measurements on the first and the second thermometer?

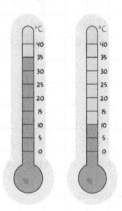

Answer _____

4. What is the temperature?

Answer _____

5. On a hot summer day the temperature was 32° Celsius. Later in the evening, the temperature rose 3.4° Celsius. What was the temperature at the night time?

A. 28.6° C
B. 35.4° C
C. 37.4° C
D. 66° C

6. What is the difference between the two measurements represented on the thermometers below?

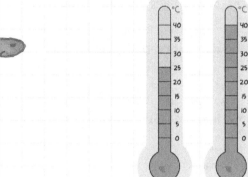

Answer _____

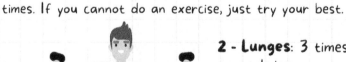

FITNESS

Please be aware of your environment and be safe at all times. If you cannot do an exercise, just try your best.

Repeat these **exercises 3 ROUNDS**

1 - Bend forward: 10 times.
Note: try to touch your feet. Make sure to keep your back straight and if needed you can bend your knees.

2 - Lunges: 3 times to each leg.
Note: Use your body weight or books as weight to do leg lunges.

3 - Plank: 6 sec.

4 - Abs: 10 times

WEEK 7 DAY 4 MATH

Temperature (Celcius) °

1. On Monday morning the temperature was 21° C. Five hours later the temperature dropped 3° C. By night time the temperature rose 4° C. What was the temperature at the night time?

   A. 9° C
   B. 14° C
   C. 22° C
   D. 28° C

2. On Thursday morning the temperature was 31° C. Six hours later the temperature dropped 6° C. By night time the temperature dropped another 2° C. What was the temperature at the night time?

   A. 23° C
   B. 25° C
   C. 37° C
   D. 39° C

3. Which tool would you use to find out how warm the tea is in a cup?

   A. Measuring cup
   B. Thermometer
   C. Teaspoon
   D. Ruler

4. What is the difference between the temperature measured in thermometer 4 and 3?

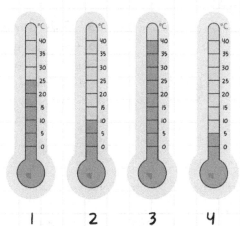

1	2	3	4

   A. 10° C
   B. 20° C
   C. 30° C
   D. 35° C

5. The temperature falls from 12° C to -1° C. How many degrees does the temperature fall?

   A. 2° C
   B. 9° C
   C. 13° C
   D. 15° C

Rewriting fractions as decimals

1. Find the fraction that is equivalent to 0.2.

   A. $\dfrac{2}{10}$

   B. $\dfrac{1}{2}$

   C. $\dfrac{20}{10}$

   D. $\dfrac{1}{4}$

2. What is $\dfrac{6}{10}$ rewritten as a decimal?

   A. 6.0
   B. 0.6
   C. 6.6
   D. 0.06

3. Which number sentence is true?

   A. $\dfrac{5}{10} = 0.2$

   B. $\dfrac{1}{3} = 0.3$

   C. $\dfrac{6}{10} = 6.1$

   D. $\dfrac{4}{10} = 0.4$

135

4. Convert the fraction $\frac{8}{10}$ into a decimal.

   A. 8.0
   B. 0.8
   C. 8.8
   D. 88

5. How can $\frac{1}{2}$ be written as a decimal?

   A. 0.2
   B. 2.2
   C. 0.5
   D. 2.0

6. Write a decimal that is equivalent to $\frac{3}{10}$.

   Answer _____

7. Convert the fraction $\frac{2}{4}$ into a decimal.

   Answer _____

8. The rope is half a meter in length. What is its length as a decimal?

   Answer _____

9. Convert the fraction $\frac{9}{10}$ into a decimal.

   Answer _____

10. Write a quarter of a meter as a decimal. Hint: What is the value of a quarter when we think about money?

   Answer _____

FITNESS

Please be aware of your environment and be safe at all times. If you cannot do an exercise, just try your best.

Repeat these exercises **3 ROUNDS**

1 - High Plank: 6 sec.

2 - Chair: 10 sec. Note: sit on an imaginary chair, keep your back straight.

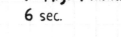
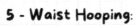

5 - Waist Hooping: 10 times. Note: if you do not have a hoop, pretend you have an imaginary hoop and rotate your hips 10 times.

4 - Abs: 10 times

3 - Side Bending: 5 times to each side. Note: try to touch your feet.

Various Real World Word related problems

1. David ran 855 yards. Jane ran 645 yards. What distance did they run altogether?

   A. 1,100 yd
   B. 1,200 yd
   C. 1,300 yd
   D. 1,500 yd

2. Rihanna had 8 days to complete her essay. How many hours did she have?

   A. 182 hours
   B. 192 hours
   C. 202 hours
   D. 212 hours

3. The apple tree had 6 times as many fruits as the peach tree. The peach tree had 45 fruits. How many fruits did the apple tree have?

   A. 250
   B. 260
   C. 270
   D. 280

4. Below is a chart showing the time it took some students to run a mile.

Student	Time (minutes)
Mason	10
Kyle	9
Sharon	12

   A. How much faster did Kyle run the mile than Sharon?

   Answer _____

   B. How much slower (in minutes) was Mason than Kyle?

   Answer _____

5. Helen baked biscuits and placed them in boxes that could contain 9 biscuits each. If she baked 180 biscuits, how many boxes did she use?

   A. 12
   B. 15
   C. 20
   D. 27

6. Robbin got to the gym at 4:15 p.m. She left the gym at 5:40 p.m. How long was she at the gym?

   Answer _____

7. Mark earns $835 per week, and Jessica earns $915 per week. How much do they earn in total per week?

   A. $1,750
   B. $1,450
   C. $1,950
   D. $1,650

8. Mary swims 7 laps every day. If she has swam 119 laps so far this month, how many days out of this month did she swim?

   A. 15 days
   B. 17 days
   C. 19 days
   D. 13 days

9. On Tuesday Saul earned $113 selling blueberry pies. On Saturday he earned $206 selling the pies. He spent $15 on buying flour and $26 buying sugar.

   A. How much money did Saul earn on these two days not including his expenses?

   Answer _____

   B. What was Saul's pure profit after his expenses?

   Answer _____

137

10. The perimeter of Isabella's square carpet is **36** feet. Help Isabella to find the area of her carpet.

    A. 76 sq ft
    B. 79 sq ft
    C. 81 sq ft
    D. 86 sq ft

11. Claire purchased a square pillow that has a perimeter of **108** inches. What is the length of one side of the pillow?

    A. 27 in
    B. 29 in
    C. 32 in
    D. 33 in

12. Lilly recorded the amount of problems she solved each week before the test. If this pattern continues, how many problems will she solve on Week 8?

Week 1	Week 2	Week 3	Week 4	Week 5
9	12	15	18	21

    A. 27
    B. 28
    C. 29
    D. 30

13. Alex set the thermostat in her house to **22°C**, which was **8°** warmer than the temperature outside. What was the temperature outside?

    Answer _____

Please be aware of your environment and be safe at all times. If you cannot do an exercise, just try your best.

1 - Down Dog: 10 sec.

2 - Bend Down: 10 sec.

3 - Chair: 10 sec.

4 - Child Pose: 20 sec.

5 - Shavasana: as long as you can. Note: think of happy moments and relax your mind.

Observing Static Charge Using Your Body

Over the last two weeks, we've seen how **magnetic charge** can help move or lift objects. This week, we're going to look at a different kind of **charge**: static electricity. Static is created when one **motion** builds up an **electrical** charge.

Materials:

 An inflated balloon (it can be inflated with oxygen or helium - either is fine)

 A plastic comb

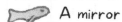 A mirror

 Note paper

Procedure:

1. Blow up the balloon and tie it closed, or get an adult to do it

2. Stand in front of the mirror and **rub the inflated balloon quickly back-and-forth across your hair** for 10 to 15 seconds to build an electrical charge.

3. Slowly lift the away from the top of your head and **observe what happens to your hair.** Move the balloon around your head to see what happens, and take note of how far you can move the balloon before it stops controlling your hair. If you want to experiment further, you can rub the balloon against your hair again to charge it back up. (**NOTE**: If you have a buzz cut or very short hair, you may want to test this on someone else in your family to observe the results better.)

4. Take 10 minutes to let the charge die down, then write down what you observed on your note paper.

5. Stand in front of the mirror again, this time with the plastic comb, and **comb your dry hair straight back, very quickly, going only one direction**. After about 15 seconds of rapid combing, lift the comb just above the front of your hair, and see what happens. Make note of this on your note sheet.

6. Take **5** more minutes to let the charge die down and answer the two questions below.

7. If you have hair on your arms or legs, you can charge the balloon up on your head one more time and see if you can use it to move your arm or leg hairs. Notice how that hair responds differently than the longer hair on top of your head.

Follow-Up Questions:

1. Based on what you saw today and what you saw over the last two weeks, how are **magnetism** and **static electricity** similar?

2. How were the effects of the **balloon** and the **comb** different?

YOGA

Please be aware of your environment and be safe at all times. If you cannot do an exercise, just try your best.

1 - Tree Pose: Stay as long as possible. Note: do on one leg then on another.

2 - Down Dog: 10 sec.

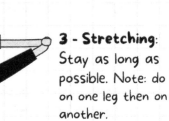

3 - Stretching: Stay as long as possible. Note: do on one leg then on another.

4 - Lower Plank: 6 sec. Note: Keep your back straight and body tight.

5 - Book Pose: 6 sec. Note: Keep your core tight. Legs should be across from your eyes.

6 - Shavasana: 5 min. Note: this pose is very important and provides you with long term benefits. Try not to skip this. Close your eyes and imagine who you want to be and what your goals are! Always think happy thoughts.

Task: Michelle is getting wet from the rain. Help her find the way through the maze so she can meet her friend Elijah who has an umbrella! Color in the pathway.

Superb!
This week we will learn about nouns, practice real-life math word problems, and learn about static charge. Let's go :)

WEEK 8

It's an octopus!
Did you know an octopus has three hearts? Two of the hearts are responsible for pumping the blood to the gills and the third heart circulates the blood around the body.

ARGOPREP

Now that you're experienced at reading and writing sentences, it's time to take your understanding of how words work to a new level! Different kinds of words do different jobs in sentences. We call those different types of words the **parts of speech**. The four most basic parts of speech that we use to create sentences are nouns, verbs, adjectives, and adverbs. We'll start by talking about **nouns**! A noun is a word that represents a person, place, or thing.

 Key Terms

Noun: A word that represents a person, place, or thing

 For Example...

A noun that represents a **person** could take the form of someone's **name**, a **job** description, or some other word that describes who or what they are.

Examples of Nouns that Represent People:		
Person	Brother	Dancer
Mr. Fernandez	Artist	Ms. Schwarz
Student	Nurse	Mom
Athlete	Francine	Goalie

In the sentence:

- <u>Mr. James</u> always eats a sandwich for lunch at the cafeteria.
- My <u>Aunt Kelly</u> was a great <u>swimmer</u> on the Stanford University team.

A noun that represents a **place** could take the form of a specific place's **name**, or it might just be a general description of the place.

Examples of Nouns that Represent Places:		
New York	Downtown	Beach
Bus Stop	Theme Park	Europe
Home	Bus Stop	California
Bedroom	City	Country

In the sentence:

◉ Mr. James always eats a sandwich for lunch at the <u>cafeteria.</u>

◉ My Aunt Kelly was a great swimmer on the <u>Stanford University</u> team.

A noun that represents a thing could take the form of a specific object's name (like a product with a brand name), or it might just be a word that represents a certain item or idea...

Examples of Nouns that Represent Things:		
Finger	Plate	Scissors
Math	Computer	Phone
Map	Ketchup	Baseball
Dog	Shoe	Pencil

In the sentence:

◉ Mr. James always eats a <u>sandwich</u> for <u>lunch</u> at the cafeteria.

◉ My Aunt Kelly was a great swimmer on the Stanford University <u>team</u>.

The Mule and the Lapdog
By Aesop

A MAN had a mule, and a Maltese Lapdog, a very great beauty. The mule was left in a stable and had plenty of oats and hay to eat, just as any other mule would. The Lapdog knew many tricks and was a great favorite with his master, who often played with him and seldom went out to dine without bringing him home some tidbit to eat.

The mule, on the contrary, had much work to do in grinding the corn-mill and in carrying wood from the forest or burdens from the farm. He often lamented his own hard fate and contrasted it with the luxury and idleness of the Lapdog, till at last one day he broke his cords and halter, and galloped into his master's house, kicking up his heels without measure, and frisking and fawning as well as he could. He next tried to jump about his master as he had seen the Lapdog do, but he broke the table and smashed all the dishes upon it to atoms. He then attempted to lick his master, and jumped upon his back.

The servants, hearing the strange hubbub and perceiving the danger of their master, quickly relieved him, and drove out the mule to his stable with kicks and clubs and cuffs. The mule, as he returned to his stall beaten nearly to death, thus lamented: "I have brought it all on myself! Why could I not have been contented to labor with my companions, and not wish to be idle all the day like that useless little Lapdog!"

1. What does the mule want at the beginning of the story?

~~~~~~

~~~~~~

2. Why is the mule jealous of the lapdog?

~~~~~~

~~~~~~

~~~~~~

~~~~~~

3. Which of these words from the first paragraph of the story is not a noun?

   A. Mule
   B. Stable
   C. Lapdog
   D. Eat

4. Why do the master's servants attack the mule when it tries to act like the lapdog?

   A. They are angry that the mule is not acting like the correct animal
   B. They are scared that he might injure or kill his master
   C. They are concerned the mule will eat all the food
   D. They are scared because they've never seen a mule before

5. Do you agree with the mule that he should've been happy to work with the other mules, rather than trying to live like a pet? Why or why not?

⭐ **Directions:**

Circle or underline the nouns in the following sentences. For each noun you find, write whether it represents a **person, place, or thing** either above or below it.

1. Our family's cat is always trying to catch mice in the basement.

2. Mr. Pew had to call a tow truck because he locked his keys in the trunk of the car.

3. The brilliant artist spent hours mixing up different colors in his studio before he started the painting.

4. The old train rattled along the tracks between New York and Philadelphia, which was a very bumpy ride for passengers.

5. In baseball, the catcher is one of the most important people in the entire stadium.

FITNESS

Please be aware of your environment and be safe at all times. If you cannot do an exercise, just try your best.

Repeat these
**exercises
3 ROUNDS**

1 - Abs:
3 times

2 - Lunges:
2 times to each leg.
Note: Use your body weight or books as weight to do leg lunges.

3 - Lunges:
3 times to each leg.
Note: Use your body weight or books as weight to do leg lunges.

5 - Plank: 6 sec.

4 - Run: 50m
Note: Run 25 meters to one side and 25 meters back to the starting position.

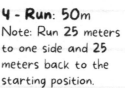

147

The Boy and the Wolf
By James Baldwin

In France there once lived a famous man who was known as the Marquis de Lafayette. When he was a little boy his mother called him Gilbert.

Gilbert de Lafayette's father and grandfather and great-grandfather had all been brave and noble men. He was very proud to think of this, and he wished that he might grow up to be like them.

His home was in the country not far from a great forest. Often, when he was a little lad, he took long walks among the trees with his mother.

"Mother," he would say, "do not be afraid. I am with you, and I will not let anything hurt you."

One day word came that a savage wolf had been seen in the forest. Men said that it was a very large wolf and that it had killed some of the farmers' sheep.

"How I should like to meet that wolf," said little Gilbert.

He was only seven years old, but now all his thoughts were about the savage beast that was in the forest.

"Shall we take a walk this morning?" asked his mother.

"Oh, yes!" said Gilbert. "Perhaps we may see that wolf among the trees.

But don't be afraid."

His mother smiled, for she felt quite sure that there was no danger.

They did not go far into the woods. The mother sat down in the shade of a tree and began to read in a new book which she had bought the day before. The boy played on the grass nearby.

The sun was warm. The bees were buzzing among the flowers. The small birds were singing softly. Gilbert looked up from his play and saw that his mother was very deeply interested in her book.

"Now for the wolf!" he said to himself.

He walked quickly, but very quietly, down the pathway into the darker woods. He looked eagerly around, but saw only a squirrel frisking among the trees and a rabbit hopping across the road.

Soon he came to a wilder place. There the bushes were very close together and the pathway came to an end. He pushed the bushes aside and went a little farther. How still everything was!

He could see a green open space just beyond; and then the woods seemed to be thicker and darker. "This is just the place for that wolf," he thought.

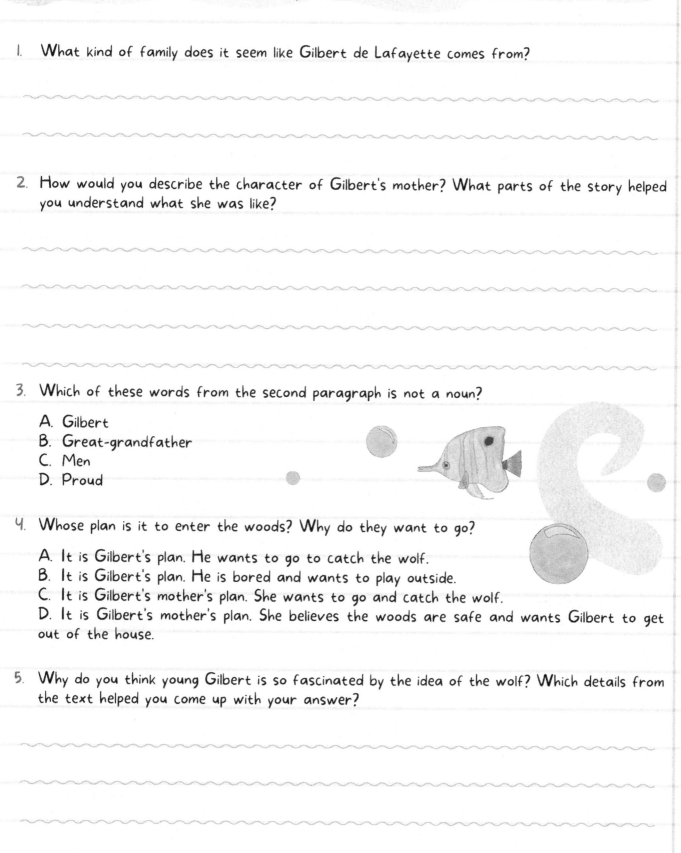

1. What kind of family does it seem like Gilbert de Lafayette comes from?

2. How would you describe the character of Gilbert's mother? What parts of the story helped you understand what she was like?

3. Which of these words from the second paragraph is not a noun?

   A. Gilbert
   B. Great-grandfather
   C. Men
   D. Proud

4. Whose plan is it to enter the woods? Why do they want to go?

   A. It is Gilbert's plan. He wants to go to catch the wolf.
   B. It is Gilbert's plan. He is bored and wants to play outside.
   C. It is Gilbert's mother's plan. She wants to go and catch the wolf.
   D. It is Gilbert's mother's plan. She believes the woods are safe and wants Gilbert to get out of the house.

5. Why do you think young Gilbert is so fascinated by the idea of the wolf? Which details from the text helped you come up with your answer?

ACTIVITIES
NOUNS

⭐ **Directions:**

Each group of words contains three nouns and two words that are not nouns. Circle or underline the words in each group that are not nouns.

1.	SQUIRREL	MIKE	READ	CHEESE	CREEPY
2.	WINTER	TENNESSEE	INTO	STADIUM	FRAMED
3.	HAPPY	HOLE	INTERNET	SAD	REFRIGERATOR
4.	ARMS	CLASSROOM	SQUID	RIDICULOUS	THROW
5.	CONFUSING	STRICT	PIANO	CANADA	APPLE

FITNESS

Please be aware of your environment and be safe at all times. If you cannot do an exercise, just try your best.

Repeat these **exercises 3 ROUNDS**

2 - Squats: 5 times. Note: imagine you are trying to sit on a chair.

3 - Side Bending: 5 times to each side. Note: try to touch your feet.

4 - Abs: 10 times

5 - Tree Pose: Stay as long as possible. Note: do the same with the other leg.

1 - High Plank: 6 sec.

Various Real World Word related problems

1. The instructions to cook a stew say to set the oven at 160ºC. If Mrs. Sanchez set her oven 12º cooler than the instructions said, what temperature did she set her oven to?

   Answer _____

2. Mr. Cooper has a pool in the shape of a rectangle. How many sides will the pool have?

   Answer _____

3. Sonora cut a piece of fabric into a shape with 5 sides. What is the name of this shape?

   Answer _____

4. Vincent created a chart showing how many points he had at the end of each level of a computer game. How would you determine the points he would have at the end of level 9?

Levels	2	3	4	5	6
Points	12	18	24	30	36

   A. Add 6 to 9
   B. Add 6 to 12
   C. Multiply 12 by 9
   D. Multiply 6 by 9

5. Garry walked $\frac{2}{5}$ of a mile on Monday and another $\frac{2}{5}$ of a mile on Tuesday. What was the total distance he walked?

   Answer _____

6. Iren's class is going to visit a museum. If each car can hold five people and there are fourteen students and 9 adults going, how many cars will they need?

   A. 3 cars
   B. 4 cars
   C. 5 cars
   D. 6 cars

7. Natalie had a piece of ribbon that measured $\frac{6}{8}$ yards in length. If she cut $\frac{2}{8}$ yards of the ribbon, what is the new length of the ribbon?

   Answer _____

8. There are 365 days in one year. How many days are in 11 years?

   Answer _____

9. A certain farm packs peaches in boxes that hold 10 each. Today the farm packed 4,820 oranges. How many boxes did they use to pack the peaches?

   Answer _____

10. An outside garbage can weighs **256** oz. A kitchen garbage can weighs **189** oz. Which weighs more and by how much?

Answer _____

11. Theatre A seated **345** people and Theatre B seated **653** people. Which theatre sat more people and by how much more?

Answer _____

12. Vicky was making herself some hot chocolate. Did she most likely use half a cup of milk or half a gallon of milk? Explain your reasoning.

Answer _____

13. Gigi bought a bottle of juice. What seems more likely? The juice was **450** milliliters or the juice was **450** liters? Explain your reasoning.

Answer _____

14. Martha purchased carrots to use in a recipe to cook for dinner for her family of four. What seems more reasonable, Martha purchased **3** pounds of carrots or **3** ounces of carrots?

Answer _____

15. Amy eats cereal in the morning. Does she most likely eat **50** grams or **5** kilograms of cereal?

Answer _____

FITNESS

Please be aware of your environment and be safe at all times. If you cannot do an exercise, just try your best.

Repeat these **exercises 3 ROUNDS**

1 - Bend forward: 10 times.
Note: try to touch your feet. Make sure to keep your back straight and if needed you can bend your knees.

2 - Lunges: 3 times to each leg.
Note: Use your body weight or books as weight to do leg lunges.

3 - Plank: 6 sec.

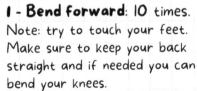

4 - Abs: 10 times

Various Real World Word related problems

The table below show the number of essays students wrote each month. Use the data to answer questions 1 - 2.

Months	Essays written per month by students
September	4
October	7
November	9
December	6

1. How many more essays were written by students in November than in September?

   A. 3
   B. 2
   C. 5
   D. 4

2. How many essays did students write in the month of October and December in total?

   Answer _____

3. Fred drew an angle of 80°. What type of angle is it?

   A. Acute
   B. Obtuse
   C. Right
   D. None of the above

4. What type of angles are in the rectangular kitchen? What is each angle measure?

   Answer _____

5. Nina baked 37 pies on Wednesday, and 69 pies on Friday. How many pies did she bake in total?

   Answer _____

A pizza cafe kept track of the different toppings they sold in a week. They recorded the results in the bar graph below. Use the graph to answer questions 6 - 7.

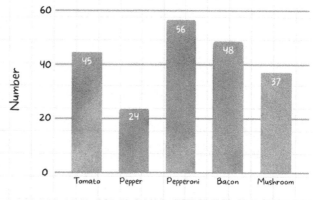

Most Sold Pizza Toppings

6. Which is the most popular topping?

   Answer _____

7. How many customers have chosen tomato or pepperoni toppings?

   Answer _____

8. Jenny cut a piece of paper that measured 8 centimeters wide and 14 centimeters long. What is the perimeter of the paper she cut out?

   A. 112 cm
   B. 44 cm
   C. 68 cm
   D. 22 cm

9. A backyard has a length of 16 meters and a total area of 144 square meters. What is the width of the backyard?

   A. 5
   B. 7
   C. 8
   D. 9

10. Liam was buying pens of different colors. He bought 17 pens at the store and he bought 19 blue pens online. How many pens did he buy in total?

    Answer _____

11. Billy bought 16 baseballs at the sports store. If each baseball cost $8 and he paid with 3 fifty dollar bills, how much change should he get back?

    A. $22
    B. $24
    C. $28
    D. $32

12. Denise spent 3 hours and 21 minutes playing computer games. If she stopped to eat dinner at 7:40 pm, what time did she start playing her computer games?

    Answer _____

FITNESS

Please be aware of your environment and be safe at all times. If you cannot do an exercise, just try your best.

Repeat these **exercises 3 ROUNDS**

1 - High Plank: 6 sec.

2 - Chair: 10 sec. Note: sit on an imaginary chair, keep your back straight.

3 - Waist Hooping: 10 times. Note: if you do not have a hoop, pretend you have an imaginary hoop and rotate your hips 10 times.

4 - Abs: 10 times

Placing fractions on a number line

1. Which fraction is missing from the number line?

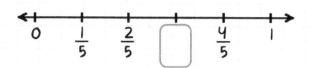

Answer _____

2. Which fraction represents one equal part of this number line?

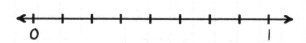

A. $\frac{1}{4}$

B. $\frac{1}{8}$

C. $\frac{1}{9}$

D. $\frac{1}{10}$

3. Find the missing fraction on the number line.

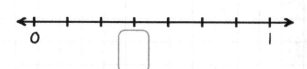

A. $\frac{3}{5}$

B. $\frac{3}{7}$

C. $\frac{3}{6}$

D. $\frac{1}{7}$

4. Where is the point on the number line?

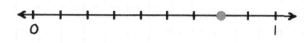

A. $\frac{1}{9}$

B. $\frac{2}{9}$

C. $\frac{7}{9}$

D. $\frac{8}{9}$

5. Find the value of k.

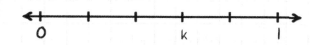

Answer _____

6. Which place on the number line is equal to the shaded part of the fraction represented in the picture below?

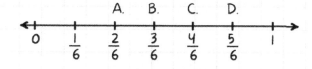

A. A, $\frac{2}{6}$

B. B, $\frac{3}{6}$

C. C, $\frac{4}{6}$

D. D, $\frac{5}{6}$

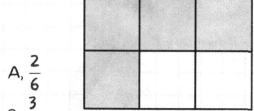

155

7. Find the missing fractions on the number line.

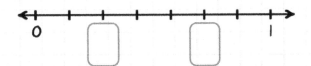

A. $\frac{2}{6}$ and $\frac{5}{6}$

B. $\frac{2}{6}$ and $\frac{4}{6}$

C. $\frac{2}{7}$ and $\frac{4}{6}$

D. $\frac{2}{7}$ and $\frac{5}{7}$

8. What fractions do the letters K and L represent on the number line?

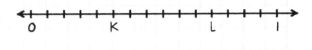

Answer _____

9. Draw the dot at $\frac{4}{10}$ on the number line.

Answer

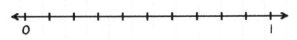

10. Which place on the number line is equal to the fraction represented in the picture below?

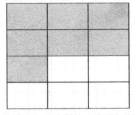

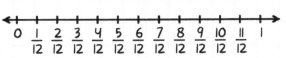

Answer _____

YOGA

Please be aware of your environment and be safe at all times. If you cannot do an exercise, just try your best.

1 - Down Dog: 10 sec.

2 - Bend Down: 10 sec.

3 - Chair: 10 sec.

4 - Child Pose: 20 sec.

5 - Shavasana: as long as you can. Note: think of happy moments and relax your mind.

WEEK 8 DAY 6   EXPERIMENT

Using a Static Charge to Move Objects

Last week, we used a **balloon** and a **comb** to build up a static charge that we could observe using our bodies. Now we'll see how static can influence the **movement** of other objects.

Materials:

- A plastic comb
- A kitchen or bathroom sink
- Two Styrofoam plates (ideally, one big one and one small one)
- A washcloth or small towel
- Note paper

Procedure:

1. First, set the plates and towel aside and **comb your hair quickly, in one direction**, over and over for **30** seconds like you did last week to build up static electricity. Your hair needs to be dry for this to work.

2. Turn on the sink, but not to full blast. You want there to be **a small, consistent stream of water** (not just drips).

3. Hold the comb vertically (straight up and down) and **move it close to the stream of water. Observe what happens when the charged-up comb comes near** the stream of water. (If nothing happens, dry off the comb, comb your hair quickly for a little longer, and try again.)

4. Turn off the sink and set the comb aside. Take the two Styrofoam plates and the washcloth to a **clean, dry**, and **flat surface**, like a counter or tabletop.

5. Put one of the Styrofoam plates (the bigger one, if you have both sizes) **face-down on the counter**.

6. Using the washcloth or small towel, **rub the bottom side of the second (small) Styrofoam plate aggressively for several seconds**. This is generating a static charge, just like when you combed your hair.

7. **Try to place the small plate on top of the large plate**, bottom side to bottom side. Observe what happens.

8. Pick the small plate back up and hold it in one hand. Open your other hand flat and hold it about 6-12 inches above the large plate with your palm down. Then, using your other hand, hold the small plate between your palm and the big plate and let go. Observe what happens and write it down on your note sheet.

Follow-Up Questions:

1. Why were combing your hair and rubbing the Styrofoam plate with the cloth such important parts of both processes?

2. Based on what you've seen over the last 4 weeks, how can a **charge** (like magnetism or static electricity) be useful for people?

YOGA

Please be aware of your environment and be safe at all times. If you cannot do an exercise, just try your best.

1 - Tree Pose: Stay as long as possible. Note: do on one leg then on another.

2 - Down Dog: 10 sec.

3 - Stretching: Stay as long as possible. Note: do on one leg then on another.

4 - Lower Plank: 6 sec. Note: Keep your back straight and body tight.

5 - Book Pose: 6 sec. Note: Keep your core tight. Legs should be across from your eyes.

6 - Shavasana: 5 min. Note: this pose is very important and provides you with long term benefits. Try not to skip this. Close your eyes and imagine who you want to be and what your goals are! Always think happy thoughts.

Task: Take a look at the eight pictures below and fill out the crossword puzzle.

Outstanding job!
In week 9 we will learn about verbs, different types of angles, number patterns, money, and more.

WEEK 9

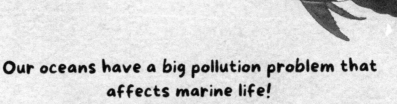

Our oceans have a big pollution problem that affects marine life!
There are billions and billions of plastic waste in our oceans from littering. Many marine life organisms can't distinguish between food and plastic, which causes harm to them.

ARGOPREP

Last week, we learned about the role of **nouns** in a sentence. Nouns are very important, but you can't create a full sentence without having a **verb** as well. Most **verbs** are **action words** that help the reader understand what the nouns in the sentence are doing or have done to them. In addition to actions, there are also **"to be" verbs**, which are usually short and used to communicate that something exists.

 Key Terms

Verb: A word that describes an action or a state something is in
Action Verb: a word that represents an action
"To Be" Verbs: The most basic verbs that communicate that something exists or is a certain way

Action Verbs

An **action verb** represents something that a person, place, or thing could do or has done to them. There's a huge variety of different action verbs!

Examples of Action Verbs		
Eat	Took	Hear
Fell	Type	Run
Swim	Throw	Cut
Explode	Talked	Fly

In a sentence:

Mr. James always <u>eats</u> a sandwich for lunch at the cafeteria.
Latisha <u>jumped</u> high to spike the volleyball.

 "To Be" Verbs

"To Be" verbs are the most basic verbs in all of the English language. They don't represent any certain action, but we use them to communicate the way things are or what quality things have.

The "To Be" Verbs		
Is	Am	Are
Was	Were	Be
Will be	Being	Been

In a sentence:

My Aunt Kelly <u>was</u> a great swimmer on the Stanford University team.
This year <u>will be</u> the best school year of all time.

The Old Woman and the Doctor
By Aesop

An old woman having lost the use of her eyes, called in a Physician to heal them, and made this bargain with him in the presence of witnesses: that if he should cure her blindness, he should receive from her a sum of money; but if her infirmity remained, she should give him nothing.

This agreement being made, the Physician, time after time, applied his salve to her eyes, and on every visit took something away, stealing all her property little by little. And when he had got all she had, he healed her and demanded the promised payment.

The Old Woman, when she recovered her sight and saw none of her goods in her house, would give him nothing. The Physician insisted on his claim, and, as she still refused, summoned her before the Judge.

The Old Woman, standing up in the Court, argued: "This man here speaks the truth in what he says; for I did promise to give him a sum of money if I should recover my sight: but if I continued blind, I was to give him nothing. Now he declares that I am healed. I on the contrary affirm that I am still blind; for when I lost the use of my eyes, I saw in my house various chattels and valuable goods: but now, though he swears I am cured of my blindness, I am not able to see a single thing in it."

1. In your own words, **summarize** the **original agreement** between the old woman and the doctor (physician)?

2. What bad or dishonorable **actions** does the physician do in the blind woman's house?

3. Which of these words from the second paragraph of the story is **not** a verb?

   A. Agreement
   B. Applied
   C. Took
   D. Healed

4. Which of these phrases from the passage contains a **"to be" verb**?

   A. "The physician, time after time, applied his salve..."
   B. "...He healed her and demanded the promised payment."
   C. "The physician insisted on his claim..."
   D. "Now he declares that I am healed..."

5. If you were the judge or a member of the jury in the court, how would you punish the physician? What **actions** would he have to take to **make up for** what he did, or how would he be **punished**?

⭐ **Directions:**

Circle or underline the **verbs** in the following sentences. For each verb you find, write whether it is an **action** or **"to be"** verb either above or below it. (**NOTE: There may be more than one verb per sentence!**)

1. Our family's cat is always trying to catch mice in the basement.

2. The old train rattled along the tracks between New York and Philadelphia, which was a very bumpy ride for passengers.

3. In baseball, the catcher is one of the most important people in the entire stadium.

4. My sister Katarina runs three miles every day, even in the winter, because she loves fitness.

5. Elephants always hold onto each other's tails with their trunks as they walk in a single-file line.

FITNESS

Please be aware of your environment and be safe at all times. If you cannot do an exercise, just try your best.

Repeat these
**exercises
3 ROUNDS**

2 - Lunges: 2 times to each leg.
Note: Use your body weight or books as weight to do leg lunges.

1 - Abs:
3 times

4 - Run: 50m
Note: Run 25 meters to one side and 25 meters back to the starting position.

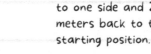

3 - Plank: 6 sec.

Another Wolf Story
By James Baldwin

The next day twenty men and boys came together for the grand wolf hunt. They tracked the beast to the mouth of a cave, far up on the hills.

They shouted and threw stones into the cave. But the wolf was too wise to show herself. She lay hidden among some rocks, and nothing could make her stir.

"I will fetch her out," said Israel Putnam.

The opening to the cave was only a narrow hole between two rocks. Putnam stooped down and looked in. It was very dark there, and he could not see anything.

Then he tied a rope around his waist and said to his friends, "Take hold of the other end, boys. When I jerk it, then pull me out as quickly as you can." He got down on his hands and knees and crawled into the cave. He crawled very slowly and carefully.

At last he saw something in the darkness that looked like two balls of fire. He knew that these were the eyes of the wolf. The wolf gave a low growl and made ready to meet him.

Putnam gave the rope a quick jerk and his friends pulled him out in great haste. They feared that the wolf was upon him; but he wished only to get his gun.

Soon, with the gun in one hand, he crept back into the cave. The wolf saw him. She growled so loudly that the men and boys outside were frightened. But Putnam was not afraid. He raised his gun and fired at the great beast. When his friends heard the gun they pulled the rope quickly and drew him out. It was no fun to be pulled over the sharp stones in that way; but it was better than to be bitten by the wolf. Putnam loaded his gun again. Then he listened. There was not a sound inside of the cave. Perhaps the wolf was waiting to spring upon him. He crept into the cave for the third time. There were no balls of fire to be seen now. No angry growl was heard. The wolf was dead.

1. Why does Israel Putnam tie a rope around his waist?

~~~~~~

~~~~~~

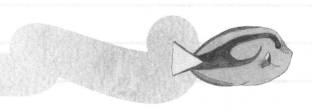

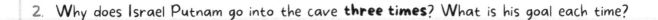
2. Why does Israel Putnam go into the cave **three times**? What is his goal each time?

3. Which of these phrases does **not** contain a verb that describes Israel's actions during the story?

   A. "...stooped down and looked in." (Paragraph 4)
   B. "...tied a rope around his waist." (Paragraph 5)
   C. "...saw something in the darkness." (Paragraph 6)
   D. "...pulled the rope quickly..." (Paragraph 8)

4. What are the "two balls of fire" described in the passage?

   A. The lanterns that Israel brings into the cave
   B. The wolf's eyes
   C. The bullets that Israel shoots at the wolf
   D. The campfires Israel and the other farmers built

5. Throughout the story, Israel Putnam performed the majority of the **actions** that led to getting rid of the wolf. Did the other men who were with him **do their part** to help, or were they unnecessary? Explain your choice!

⭐ **Directions:**

Each group of words contains **three verbs** and **two words that are not verbs**. Circle or underline the words in each group that are <u>not</u> verbs.

1. SMELL	THINK	TOAD	COUGH	AIRPLANE
2. WAVE	TACO	WHISPER	PLAY	SCREWDRIVER
3. ARTIST	VALENTINE	SIT	TACKLE	TOSS
4. SLITHER	GOLDFISH	PRINT	PRINTER	CHEW
5. MOUSE	READ	SEPTEMBER	OPEN	LAUGH

FITNESS

Please be aware of your environment and be safe at all times. If you cannot do an exercise, just try your best.

Repeat these **exercises 3 ROUNDS**

3 - Side Bending: 5 times to each side. Note: try to touch your feet.

4 - Abs: 10 times

2 - Squats: 5 times. Note: imagine you are trying to sit on a chair.

5 - Tree Pose: Stay as long as possible. Note: do the same with the other leg.

1 - High Plank: 6 sec.

Right, Acute, Obtuse Angles

1. Look at the angle marked on this shape:

What type of angle is this?

A. Acute
B. Obtuse
C. Right
D. None of the above

2. What type of marked angle is on this shape?

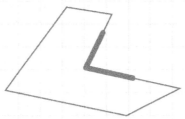

A. Acute
B. Obtuse
C. Right
D. None of the above

Use the figures below to answer questions 3 - 5.

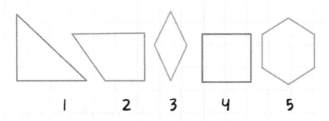

3. Which figures have at least one acute angle?

Answer _____

4. Which figures have at least one obtuse angle?

Answer _____

5. Which figures have at least one right angle?

Answer _____

6. Is this angle greater than, equal to, or less than a right angle?

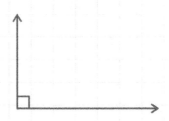

A. Greater than a right angle
B. Equal to a right angle
C. Less than a right angle

7. Is this angle greater than, equal to, or less than a right angle?

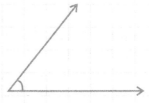

A. Greater than a right angle
B. Equal to a right angle
C. Less than a right angle

Use the drawing below to answer questions 8 - 10.

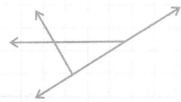

8. How many acute angles are in the diagram above?

Answer _____

9. How many obtuse angles are in the diagram?

Answer _____

10. How many right angles are in the diagram?

Answer _____

More rounding problems

1. Round **2,689** to the nearest thousand.

   A. 2,680
   B. 2,700
   C. 2,000
   D. 3,000

2. Round **1,345** to the nearest hundred.

   Answer _____

3. Determine a number that fills in the blank. _____ rounded to the nearest ten is **260**.

   A. 269
   B. 261
   C. 273
   D. 248

4. Use the number line to round number 163 to the nearest 10.

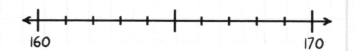

   Answer _____

FITNESS

Please be aware of your environment and be safe at all times. If you cannot do an exercise, just try your best.

Repeat these **exercises 3 ROUNDS**

1 - Bend forward: 10 times.
Note: try to touch your feet. Make sure to keep your back straight and if needed you can bend your knees.

2 - Lunges: 3 times to each leg.
Note: Use your body weight or books as weight to do leg lunges.

3 - Plank: 6 sec.

4 - Abs: 10 times

More rounding problems

1. Use the number line to round the number **678** to the nearest **100**.

```
←|||||||||||||||||||||||||||||||||||||||||||||||||||||||→
600                                              700
```

Answer _____

2. Which of the following numbers rounded to the nearest thousand gives you **5,000**?

   A. 5,432
   B. 5,564
   C. 4,398
   D. 4,449

3. What is **2,348** rounded to the nearest ten?

   A. 2,340
   B. 2,350
   C. 2,400
   D. 2,000

4. Which of the following numbers rounded to the nearest hundred gives you **3,600**?

   A. 3,690
   B. 3,450
   C. 3,524
   D. 3,586

5. Which place value should you round in the number **3,783** to get **4,000**?

Answer _____

6. Which place value should you round in the number **2,734** to get **2,700**?

Answer _____

Patterns and Rules

1. Determine what rule the pattern is using.
   3, 6, 12, 24, 48, ...

   A. Add 3
   B. Add 6
   C. Times 2
   D. Times 3

2. The number pattern is "add 9". Which number is next: **2, 11, 20, 29, ...?**

   A. 36
   B. 37
   C. 38
   D. 39

3. Find the rule if the numbers in the pattern are: **16, 29, 42, 55, ...**

   A. Add 16
   B. Times 16
   C. Add 13
   D. Times 2

4. Take a look at the following numbers: **4, 15, 26, 37.** If the pattern continues what will be the 8th number in the pattern?

   A. 76
   B. 81
   C. 89
   D. 94

5. What rule is used for the pattern **1, 6, 36, 216, ...?**

   A. Add 5
   B. Times 5
   C. Add 6
   D. Times 6

6. Look at the pattern below. What might the next shape look like?

Answer _____

_____

7. The rule for the pattern shown below is "+ 7". Fill in the missing numbers.

9, ..., 23, 30, ..., 44

Answer _____

8. Start at 25 and create a pattern with the rule add 18. What is the fourth number in the pattern?

Answer _____

9. Oliver listed these numbers: 3, 12, 48, 192. What rule did Oliver use?

Answer _____

10. Look at the pattern 9, ..., 36, ..., 144. The number pattern is "times 2". What is the missing numbers?

Answer _____

FITNESS

Please be aware of your environment and be safe at all times. If you cannot do an exercise, just try your best.

Repeat these exercises **3 ROUNDS**

1 - High Plank: 6 sec.

2 - Chair: 10 sec. Note: sit on an imaginary chair, keep your back straight.

3 - Waist Hooping: 10 times. Note: if you do not have a hoop, pretend you have an imaginary hoop and rotate your hips 10 times.

4 - Abs: 10 times

Money

1. Jake lost **$102**. Lillian lost **$67**. Who lost more money? Prove your answer.

Answer _____

2. How much money is shown below?

A. $1 and 30¢
B. $1 and 80¢
C. $2 and 30¢
D. $2

3. Determine the amount of money shown below.

A. $58
B. $68
C. $78
D. $88

4. How much money is there?

A. $22 and 83¢
B. $22 and 88¢
C. $23 and 28¢
D. $23 and 8¢

5. Determine which choice best describes the coins in the order shown.

A. nickel, quarter, penny, dime
B. nickel, dime, quarter, penny
C. quarter, dime, penny, nickel
D. dime, nickel, quarter, penny

6. Determine the amount of money shown below.

A. $25 and 35¢
B. $25 and 40¢
C. $15 and 50¢
D. $15 and 53¢

7. Which statement is true?

A. 1 dollar = 50 nickels
B. 2 dollars = 25 dimes
C. 30 cents = 6 nickels
D. 1 dime = 20 cents

8. Which statement is FALSE?

A. 2 dollars = 20 dimes
B. 3 dollars = 300 cents
C. 150 cents = 6 quarters
D. 15 dimes = 80 nickels

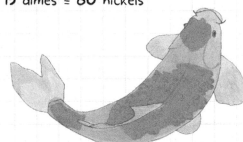

9. Complete the table to show equivalent measurements in dollars and cents.

Dollars	Cents
1/2	
1/4	
3	

10. How much money is shown below?

Answer _____

11. Katie took a train from her house to the state capitol. She paid **$2** for the train ticket. How much will she have spent in total on train tickets if she takes the same train back home?

Answer _____

12. What is $14 and 64¢ + $15 and 42¢?

A. $29 and 6¢
B. $30 and 6¢
C. $31 and 6¢
D. $31 and 16¢

13. What is 12 dollars and 16 cents subtracted from 28 dollars and 82 cents ?

A. 17 dollars and 36 cents
B. 16 dollars and 56 cents
C. 16 dollars and 66 cents
D. 15 dollars and 86 cents

YOGA

Please be aware of your environment and be safe at all times. If you cannot do an exercise, just try your best.

2 - Bend Down: 10 sec.

1 - Down Dog: 10 sec.

3 - Chair: 10 sec.

4 - Child Pose: 20 sec.

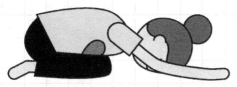

5 - Shavasana: as long as you can. Note: think of happy moments and relax your mind.

Recognizing Inherited Traits

All organisms, animals, and plants have what we call **traits**. Traits are **characteristic features that we can observe**. That's a fancy way of saying that a "trait" is an aspect or detail of someone or something that we can see. Traits come from a variety of different places. Some traits you are **born with** because of your parents, some traits are **acquired** during life, and other traits are **the result of where and how you live**.

This week, we're going to focus on **inherited traits** - the traits you get from your parents. This activity involves looking at traits that exist within your family. If you're adopted or don't live with your genetic parents, you can still do this activity, though! Just ask whoever you live with for some family photos and you can observe traits in their family.

Materials:

 Family photos - the more the better (preferably showing at least **3** generations - for example: grandparents, parents, kids, etc.)

 Note paper

 Your parents, grandparents, or guardians

Procedure:

1. First **lay out a collection of family pictures on a tabletop and study each one**. On your note paper, write down what traits you observe about each person in the photos: What is their body type? What color or kind of hair do they have? What shape are their ears, noses, chins, etc.?

2. With the help of your parents, grandparents, or guardians, **identify all the people in the photos and create a family tree**, if necessary.

3. Review your notes and look for **shared traits** - Do two members of your family have really similar noses or the exact same curly hair? Make a list of traits that different members of your family share.

4. Ask your parents, grandparents, or guardians to **review your list of shared traits and add any others that they can think of**.

5. Answer the questions below and then clean up your family pictures.

Follow-Up Questions:

1. What was one **inherited, physical trait** that you observed in your family?

~~~~~~

~~~~~~

~~~~~~

2. If you have children in the future, what's **a trait from your family that you hope they have**, based on what you just observed?

~~~~~~

~~~~~~

~~~~~~

YOGA

Please be aware of your environment and be safe at all times. If you cannot do an exercise, just try your best.

1 - Tree Pose: Stay as long as possible. Note: do on one leg then on another.

2 - Down Dog: 10 sec.

3 - Stretching: Stay as long as possible. Note: do on one leg then on another.

5 - Book Pose: 6 sec. Note: Keep your core tight. Legs should be across from your eyes.

6 - Shavasana: 5 min. Note: this pose is very important and provides you with long term benefits. Try not to skip this. Close your eyes and imagine who you want to be and what your goals are! Always think happy thoughts.

4 - Lower Plank: 6 sec. Note: Keep your back straight and body tight.

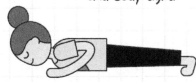

Task: Help complete this jigsaw puzzle. There are five pieces missing. Which of the pieces belong to the respective letters?

Wow!

You sure are impressive. This week we will learn about subject & predicate, and continue practicing angles and money-related word problems.

WEEK 10

It's a seal!

Seals are semiaquatic marine mammals that have a lifespan of 15 to 40 years depending on the species. Some species of seals, such as elephant seals, can hold their breath underwater for 2 hours!

ARGOPREP

Now that you know about **nouns** and **verbs**, you can gain a higher understanding of how sentences are put together. A sentence is broken up into two main parts: the **subject**, which contains the **nouns** that the sentence is mainly about, and the **predicate**, which contains all the information about either what the subject did or what happened to the subject in the sentence.

Key Terms

Subject: The part of the sentence that tells you **who** or **what** the sentence is about
Predicate: The part of the sentence that tells you **what happened**

Identifying Subjects & Predicates

When you read a sentence, try to find the spot where the sentence switches from **telling you who or what it's about** to **telling you what happened**. That's the dividing line between the subject and the predicate!

HINT: The first word of the predicate is almost always the main verb of the sentence.

 For Example...

◉ My brother and I played basketball at the park.

   🐚 SUBJECT: My brother and I **(That's who the sentence is about!)**
   🐚 PREDICATE: ...played basketball at the park. **(That's what the subject did)**

◉ The submarine full of sailors dove down beneath the waves.

   🐚 SUBJECT: The submarine full of sailors **(That's what the sentence is about!)**
   🐚 PREDICATE: ...dove down beneath the waves. **(That's what the subject did)**

◉ My crummy old cell phone's battery never lasts more than a few hours.

   🐚 SUBJECT: My crummy old cell phone's battery **(That's what the sentence is about!)**
   🐚 PREDICATE: ...never lasts more than a few hours. **(That's what the subject does - or doesn't do!)**

◉ Everybody in the bus got in trouble for being too loud.

   🐚 SUBJECT: Everybody on the bus **(That's who the sentence is about!)**
   🐚 PREDICATE: ...got in trouble for being too loud. **(That's what happened to the subject)**

The Stag in the Ox Stall
By Aesop

A stag, roundly chased by the hounds and blinded by fear to the danger he was running into, took shelter in a farmyard and hid himself in a shed among the oxen. An Ox gave him this kindly warning: "O unhappy creature! why should you thus, of your own accord, incur destruction and trust yourself in the house of your enemy?"

The Stag replied: "Only allow me, friend, to stay where I am, and I will undertake to find some favorable opportunity of effecting my escape."

At the approach of the evening the herdsman came to feed his cattle, but did not see the Stag; and even the farm-bailiff with several laborers passed through the shed and failed to notice him. The Stag, congratulating himself on his safety, began to express his sincere thanks to the Oxen who had kindly helped him in the hour of need.

One of them again answered him: "We indeed wish you well, but the danger is not over. There is one other yet to pass through the shed, who has as it were a hundred eyes, and until he has come and gone, your life is still in peril."

At that moment the master himself entered, and having had to complain that his oxen had not been properly fed, he went up to their racks and cried out: "Why is there such a scarcity of fodder? There is not half enough straw for them to lie on. Those lazy fellows have not even swept the cobwebs away."

While he thus examined everything in turn, he spied the tips of the antlers of the Stag peeping out of the straw. Then summoning his laborers, he ordered that the Stag should be seized and killed.

1. **Why** does the stag wind up in the farm shed at the beginning of the story?

2. How would you describe the **stag's personality**? Provide at least **three details**.

3. Which of these examples correctly divides the sentence from the text into its subject and predicate?

   A. Those / lazy fellows have not even swept the cobwebs away.
   B. Those lazy fellows / have not even swept the cobwebs away.
   C. Those lazy fellows have not even / swept the cobwebs away.
   D. Those lazy fellows have not even swept / the cobwebs away.

4. Why do the animals in the shed say the master has "a hundred eyes?"

   A. The master is some sort of monster
   B. The master has a whole team of workers who help him look for things
   C. They have never actually seen the master and have only heard legends about him
   D. The master is very observant

5. **How** could the stag have **acted differently** to prevent the farmer from catching it?

   ~~~~~~

   ~~~~~~

   ~~~~~~

   ~~~~~~

   ~~~~~~

   ~~~~~~

⭐ **Directions:**

Circle the **subject** in each sentence below. Then, underline the **predicate**. (**REMEMBER: The predicate <u>usually</u> starts with the main verb!**)

1. Dr. Shapiro has been my pediatrician since I was born.

2. We will learn much more about the universe if we ever communicate with aliens.

3. Almost none of the cars in the race finished because there were several major crashes.

4. Clyde and Christopher can't seem to stay out of trouble for long.

5. My dad's truck broke down on the drive to school, which is why I was late.

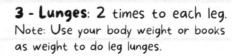

FITNESS

Please be aware of your environment and be safe at all times. If you cannot do an exercise, just try your best.

Repeat these
exercises
3 ROUNDS

3 - Lunges: 2 times to each leg.
Note: Use your body weight or books as weight to do leg lunges.

4 - Bend forward: 10 times.
Note: try to touch your feet. Make sure to keep your back straight and if needed you can bend your knees.

2 - Abs:
3 times

5 - Run: 50m
Note: Run 25 meters to one side and 25 meters back to the starting position.

1 - Plank: 6 sec.

A Lesson in Manners
By James Baldwin

One morning there was a loud knock at Dean Swift's door. The servant opened it. A man who was outside handed her a fine duck that had lately been killed, and said, - "Here's a present for the Dean. It's from Mr. Boyle."

Then, without another word, he turned and walked away.

A few days afterward the man came again. This time he brought a partridge. "Here's another bird from Mr. Boyle."

Now, Mr. Boyle was a sporting neighbor who spent a good deal of time in shooting. He was a great admirer of Dean Swift, and took pleasure in sending him presents of game.

The third time, the man brought a quail. "Here's something else for the Dean," he said roughly, and tossed it into the servant's arms.

The servant complained to her master. "That fellow has no manners," she said.

"The next time he comes," said the Dean, "let me know, and I will go to the door."

It was not long until the man came with another present. The Dean went to the door.

"Here's a rabbit from Mr. Boyle," said the man.

"See here," said the Dean in a stern voice, "that is not the way to deliver a message here. Just step inside and make believe that you are Dean Swift. I will go out and make believe that I am bringing him a present. I will show you how a messenger ought to behave."

"I'll agree to that," said the man; and he stepped inside. The Dean took the rabbit and went out of the house. He walked up the street to the next block. Then he came back and knocked gently at the door.

The door was opened by the man from Mr. Boyle's. The Dean bowed gracefully and said, "If you please, sir, Mr. Boyle's compliments, and he wishes you to accept of this fine rabbit."

"Oh, thank you," said the man very politely. Then, taking out his purse, he offered the Dean a shilling. "And here is something for your trouble."

I. How does Dean Swift teach the bird delivery man the right way to behave?

⭐ **Directions:**

Circle the **subject** in each sentence below. Then, underline the **predicate**. (**REMEMBER: The predicate <u>usually</u> starts with the main verb!**)

1. Dr. Shapiro has been my pediatrician since I was born.

2. We will learn much more about the universe if we ever communicate with aliens.

3. Almost none of the cars in the race finished because there were several major crashes.

4. Clyde and Christopher can't seem to stay out of trouble for long.

5. My dad's truck broke down on the drive to school, which is why I was late.

FITNESS

Please be aware of your environment and be safe at all times. If you cannot do an exercise, just try your best.

Repeat these **exercises 3 ROUNDS**

3 - Lunges: 2 times to each leg.
Note: Use your body weight or books as weight to do leg lunges.

4 - Bend forward: 10 times.
Note: try to touch your feet. Make sure to keep your back straight and if needed you can bend your knees.

2 - Abs:
3 times

1 - Plank: 6 sec.

5 - Run: 50m
Note: Run 25 meters to one side and 25 meters back to the starting position.

181

A Lesson in Manners
By James Baldwin

One morning there was a loud knock at Dean Swift's door. The servant opened it. A man who was outside handed her a fine duck that had lately been killed, and said, - "Here's a present for the Dean. It's from Mr. Boyle."

Then, without another word, he turned and walked away.

A few days afterward the man came again. This time he brought a partridge. "Here's another bird from Mr. Boyle."

Now, Mr. Boyle was a sporting neighbor who spent a good deal of time in shooting. He was a great admirer of Dean Swift, and took pleasure in sending him presents of game.

The third time, the man brought a quail. "Here's something else for the Dean," he said roughly, and tossed it into the servant's arms.

The servant complained to her master. "That fellow has no manners," she said.

"The next time he comes," said the Dean, "let me know, and I will go to the door."

It was not long until the man came with another present. The Dean went to the door.

"Here's a rabbit from Mr. Boyle," said the man.

"See here," said the Dean in a stern voice, "that is not the way to deliver a message here. Just step inside and make believe that you are Dean Swift. I will go out and make believe that I am bringing him a present. I will show you how a messenger ought to behave."

"I'll agree to that," said the man; and he stepped inside. The Dean took the rabbit and went out of the house. He walked up the street to the next block. Then he came back and knocked gently at the door.

The door was opened by the man from Mr. Boyle's. The Dean bowed gracefully and said, "If you please, sir, Mr. Boyle's compliments, and he wishes you to accept of this fine rabbit."

"Oh, thank you," said the man very politely. Then, taking out his purse, he offered the Dean a shilling. "And here is something for your trouble."

1. How does Dean Swift teach the bird delivery man the right way to behave?

2. **Why** does Dean Swift's servant say that the man who delivers the birds has "no manners?"

3. Which of these examples correctly divides the sentence from the text into its subject and predicate?

   A. Now, / Mr. Boyle was a sporting neighbor who spent a good deal of time in shooting.
   B. Now, Mr. Boyle / was a sporting neighbor who spent a good deal of time in shooting.
   C. Now, Mr. Boyle was a sporting neighbor / who spent a good deal of time in shooting.
   D. Now, Mr. Boyle was a sporting neighbor who /spent a good deal of time in shooting.

4. Which of these things does the delivery man **not** bring Dean Swift in the story?

   A. A duck
   B. A partridge
   C. A turkey
   D. A rabbit

5. How does **the bird delivery man** teach Dean Swift a **lesson of his own?**

⭐ **Directions:**

Somebody already tried to separate the sentences below into their **subjects** and **predicates**, but they definitely messed a few of them up! Let's double-check their work. If the line that divides the subject and the predicate is in the right place, write **CORRECT** on the line below the sentence. If the sentence is divided in the wrong place, write **INCORRECT** below and use your pen or pencil to **draw in a new line** that shows where the subject ends and the predicate begins.

1. My Uncle Ted works / at a power plant.

2. The English language / is considered very difficult to learn because it is complicated.

3. A flying V of Canadian geese passed loudly / over the house.

4. Many people are / afraid of flying in planes.

5. Everybody who has known me since I was young says that / I am the same now as I always have been.

FITNESS

Please be aware of your environment and be safe at all times. If you cannot do an exercise, just try your best.

Repeat these **exercises 3 ROUNDS**

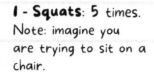

1 - Squats: 5 times. Note: imagine you are trying to sit on a chair.

2 - Side Bending: 5 times to each side. Note: try to touch your feet.

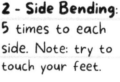

3 - Tree Pose: Stay as long as possible. Note: do the same with the other leg.

WEEK 10 DAY 3 🦭 MATH

Money

1. Rachel loves eating fruits. She paid $18 and 71¢ for berries, and $17 and 8¢ for avocados. In total, how much money did Rachel spend?

   Answer _____

2. Edward bought 8 pencils at a store. If each pencil cost $2 and 11¢ and he paid with a twenty dollar bill, how much change should he get back?

   Answer _____

3. Neil went to the mall on Thursday to buy clothes. He spent $16 and 36¢ on shorts and $12 and 93¢ on a T-shirt. In total, how much money did Neil spend on clothes?

   Answer _____

4. On Friday, Sandra bought two movie tickets each costing $13 and 67 cents. She also borrowed 6 DVDs which each cost $7. How much more money did Sandra spend on the DVDs than the movie tickets?

   Answer _____

5. Find the result of subtracting 344 dollars and 50 cents from 964 dollars.

   Answer _____

6. Mr. Harrison bought 15 copybooks at the store. If each copybook cost $4 and 81¢ and he paid with a hundred dollar bill, how much change should he get back?

   Answer _____

7. Complete an addition statement $45 and 67¢ + ___¢ = $46 and 51¢.

   Answer _____

Angles

1. Look at the angle marked on this shape:

   What type of angle is it?

   A. Acute
   B. Obtuse
   C. Right
   D. None of the above

2. Look at the angle marked on this shape:

   What type of angle is it?

   A. Acute
   B. Obtuse
   C. Right
   D. None of the above

3. What type of angles does a ruler have?

A. Acute
B. Obtuse
C. Right
D. None of the above

4. What type of angles does a pentagon have if all its sides are equal?

Answer _____

5. Count the total number of Acute angles for all the shapes below.

A. 6
B. 7
C. 8
D. 9

6. Count the total number of Obtuse angles for all the shapes below.

A. 5
B. 6
C. 7
D. 8

7. Count the number of Right angles for all shapes below.

A. 4
B. 5
C. 6
D. 7

FITNESS

Repeat these exercises **3 ROUNDS**

Please be aware of your environment and be safe at all times. If you cannot do an exercise, just try your best.

1 - Bend forward: 10 times.
Note: try to touch your feet. Make sure to keep your back straight and if needed you can bend your knees.

2 - Lunges: 3 times to each leg.
Note: Use your body weight or books as weight to do leg lunges.

3 - Plank: 6 sec.

4 - Abs: 10 times

Angles

1. There is an angle that measures 110°. What type of angle is it?

   A. Acute
   B. Obtuse
   C. Right
   D. None of the above

2. There is an angle that measures 36°. What type of angle is it?

   A. Acute
   B. Obtuse
   C. Right
   D. None of the above

3. There is an angle that measures 90°. What type of angle is it?

   A. Acute
   B. Obtuse
   C. Right
   D. None of the above

4. Identify each angle of the shape below. Which of them is acute, obtuse and right?

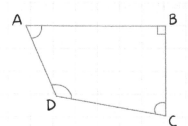

   A. _____
   B. _____
   C. _____
   D. _____

5. Tick the box that applies to this angle.

Angle	Acute	Obtuse	Right

6. Classify each angle as acute, obtuse or right.

   A. 90° _____
   B. 87° _____
   C. 160° _____
   D. 95° _____

7. Is this angle less than, equal to, or greater than a right angle?

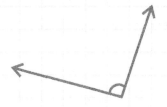

   Answer _____

8. Tick the box that applies to this angle.

Angle	Acute	Obtuse	Right

9. Is this angle less than, equal to, or greater than a right angle?

Answer _____

10. For the figure below, count the number of angles of each type.

A. Number of acute angles _____

B. Number of obtuse angles _____

C. Number of right angles _____

11. What is the measurement of this angle? Choose the best estimate.

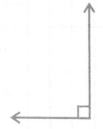

A. 45°
B. 60°
C. 90°
D. 120°

12. What is the measurement of this angle? Choose the best estimate.

A. 45°
B. 90°
C. 120°
D. 145°

13. For the figure below, count the number of angles of each type.

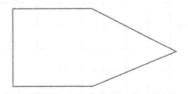

A. Number of acute angles _____

B. Number of obtuse angles _____

C. Number of right angles _____

FITNESS

Repeat these exercises **3 ROUNDS**

Please be aware of your environment and be safe at all times. If you cannot do an exercise, just try your best.

1 - High Plank: 6 sec.

2 - Chair: 10 sec.
Note: sit on an imaginary chair, keep your back straight.

3 - Waist Hooping: 10 times. Note: if you do not have a hoop, pretend you have an imaginary hoop and rotate your hips 10 times.

4 - Abs: 10 times

Round the following number to the place indicated below

1. 5,795,78<u>4</u>.7

   A. 5,795,786
   B. 5,795,785
   C. 5,795,784
   D. 5,795,784.7

2. 74,45<u>8</u>.2

   A. 74,459
   B. 74,460
   C. 74,458
   D. 74,457

3. 82,958,<u>0</u>03

   A. 82,958,700
   B. 82,957,000
   C. 82,958,100
   D. 82,958,000

4. 6<u>7</u>0

   A. 700
   B. 800
   C. 670
   D. 600

5. 7,9<u>6</u>0

   A. 7,964
   B. 7,970
   C. 7,960
   D. 7,950

Let's learn about place values! Look at the number that is underlined and determine its place value.

6. 47<u>4</u>,815

   A. hundreds
   B. thousands
   C. ten-thousandths
   D. hundredths

7. 15,6<u>4</u>2,510

   A. thousands
   B. thousandths
   C. hundred thousands
   D. ten thousands

8. 2,421,5<u>0</u>4

   A. ones
   B. tens
   C. thousands
   D. hundredths

9. 83<u>9</u>,897

   A. thousandths
   B. tenths
   C. hundredths
   D. thousands

10. 6,8<u>0</u>2,536

   A. tenths
   B. thousands
   C. tens
   D. ones

Multiplication Drills:

11. -10×-8

   A. 83
   B. -18
   C. 84
   D. 80

12. 3×-10

   A. -7
   B. -30
   C. -27
   D. -26

13. 12 × -6

    A. -96
    B. 96
    C. -72
    D. -70

14. -4 × 2

    A. -8
    B. -18
    C. -1
    D. -12

15. -10 × -1

    A. -10
    B. 0
    C. 7
    D. 10

Addition and Subtraction Drills:

16. 1 + 16

    A. 33
    B. 17
    C. 65
    D. 26

17. 74 + 82

    A. 156
    B. 138
    C. 130
    D. 201

18. 82 + 28

    A. 106
    B. 96
    C. 36
    D. 110

19. 1 + 50

    A. 33
    B. 51
    C. 94
    D. 82

20. 38 - 12

    A. 26
    B. 36
    C. 77
    D. 118

YOGA

Please be aware of your environment and be safe at all times. If you cannot do an exercise, just try your best.

1 - Down Dog: 10 sec.

2 - Bend Down: 10 sec.

3 - Chair: 10 sec.

4 - Child Pose: 20 sec.

5 - Shavasana: as long as you can. Note: think of happy moments and relax your mind.

WEEK 10 DAY 6  EXPERIMENT

How Environment Affects Traits

Last week, we took a look at **inherited traits** - characteristics that we get from our ancestors. This week, we'll be thinking about how **environment** affects traits. The environment is the area or place in which a certain organism lives.

Materials:

 One piece of regular paper

 Scissors

 A hat, bag, or bowl

 A pen

 Encyclopedias or internet access (for research)

 Note paper

 Art supplies (crayons, colored pens, pencils, etc.)

Procedure:

1. First, cut a plain sheet of paper into **5** pieces and use a pen to label each one **"TUNDRA"**, **"DECIDUOUS FOREST"**, **"RAIN FOREST"**, **"DESERT"**, and **"GRASSLAND"**. Fold the pieces of paper up and place them into the bowl, bag, or hat.

2. Stir the pieces of paper around and **select one at random**. You have just chosen a climate zone/environment.

3. Using your encyclopedia or the internet, **take 30 minutes to research the type of environment you just selected**. Try to figure out what that area is like, how easy or hard it is to find food there, and what challenges the animals who live their face. Use your note paper to keep track of this information.

4. Using your imagination, **brainstorm a new animal** that could live in that environment. Think about **what traits** an animal would need to thrive in that environment. You can use other animals who already live there to find inspiration, but try to create something that is truly new.

5. Using your art supplies, **draw a picture of your new animal** that displays the traits you think are important for survival in the environment you chose.

6. **Label each trait, then write a one-sentence explanation** of how it will help your animal thrive.

7. Once you've created your new animal, drawn your picture, and labeled it, answer the questions below. Then, if you want, you can pull another environment out of the hat or bowl and create another new animal!

Follow-Up Questions:

1. How can an animal or organism's environment affect its traits?

~~~~~~

~~~~~~

~~~~~~

2. Give an example of a trait that will help the animal you created live effectively in the environment you chose.

~~~~~~

~~~~~~

~~~~~~

YOGA

Please be aware of your environment and be safe at all times. If you cannot do an exercise, just try your best.

1 - Tree Pose: Stay as long as possible. Note: do on one leg then on another.

2 - Down Dog: 10 sec.

3 - Stretching: Stay as long as possible. Note: do on one leg then on another.

4 - Lower Plank: 6 sec. Note: Keep your back straight and body tight.

5 -Book Pose: 6 sec. Note: Keep your core tight. Legs should be across from your eyes.

6 - Shavasana: 5 min. Note: this pose is very important and provides you with long term benefits. Try not to skip this. Close your eyes and imagine who you want to be and what your goals are! Always think happy thoughts.

Task: There are five pieces missing from this jigsaw puzzle. Match the missing letters with the corresponding number.

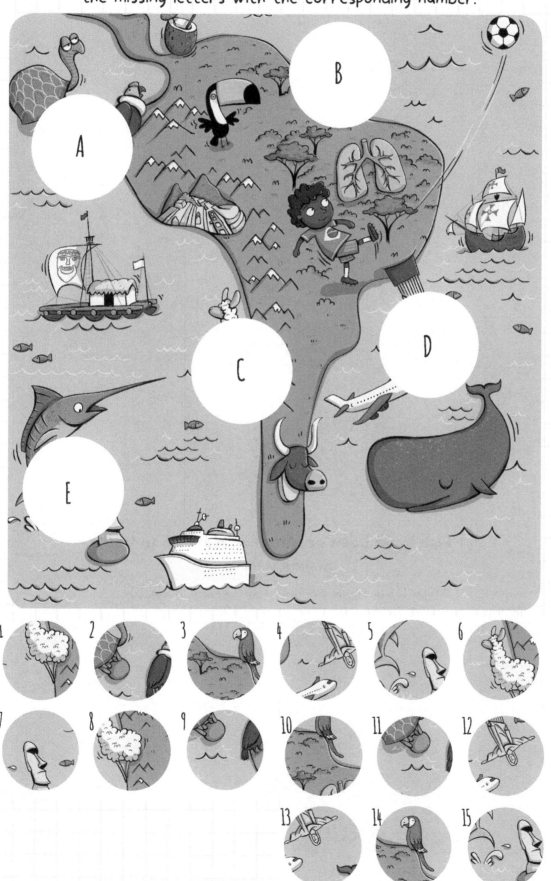

WEEK 11

Impressive!
Get ready to learn about adjectives and practice various math concepts that we have covered in the previous weeks.

Fish have been around for more than 450 million years!

Fish have been around far before dinosaurs roamed the earth.

ARGOPREP

Nouns and **verbs** are the two most basic parts of speech, but you've probably noticed that we need a lot more words to make an interesting sentence. **Adjectives** are words that spice up writing by making the nouns more descriptive. With a strong understanding of adjectives, you can write more complex sentences and keep your readers hooked by providing great details!

 Key Terms

Adjective: A word that describes or modifies a noun
Noun: A word that represents a person, place, or thing

For Example...

Adjectives can give us all sorts of information about nouns. They can tell us about the **size** of something, what **color** it is, what **shape** it is, or what it's **made from**. When we're describing **people**, adjectives help us describe what they **look like** and how their **personalities** are.

Examples of Adjectives		
Big	Yellow	Metallic
Slippery	Smart	Excited
Nervous	Thin	Tired
Smelly	Wooden	Old fashioned

In the sentence:

- An <u>annoying</u> mosquito kept buzzing around my head.
  - **Annoying** is an adjective that describes the **mosquito**
    - It tells you about the mosquito's **personality** and how the speaker of the sentence feels about it

- The <u>plastic</u> toy began to melt on the <u>hot</u> pavement.
  - **Plastic** is an adjective that describes the **toy**
    - It tells you what it's **made of**
  - **Hot** is an adjective that describes the **pavement**
    - It tells you **what the pavement feels like**

- Mrs. Fischer gave us a <u>surprise</u> quiz because she is <u>evil</u>.
  - **Surprise** is an adjective that describes the **quiz**
    - It tells you **what kind** of a quiz it was
  - **Evil** is an adjective that describes **Mrs. Fischer**
    - It tells you how Mrs. Fischer's students feel about her personality

The Mice and the Weasels
By Aesop

The Weasels and the Mice waged a perpetual war with each other, in which much blood was shed. The Weasels were always the victors.

The Mice thought that the cause of their frequent defeats was that they had no leaders set apart from the general army to command them, and that they were exposed to dangers from lack of discipline. They therefore chose as leaders Mice that were most renowned for their family descent, strength, and counsel, as well as those most noted for their courage in the fight, so that they might be better marshaled in battle array and formed into troops, regiments, and battalions.

When all this was done, and the army disciplined, and the herald Mouse had duly proclaimed war by challenging the Weasels, the newly chosen generals bound their heads with straws, that they might be more conspicuous to all their troops.

Scarcely had the battle begun, when a great rout overwhelmed the Mice, who scampered off as fast as they could to their holes. The generals, not being able to get in on account of the ornaments on their heads, were all captured and eaten by the Weasels.

The more honor the more danger.

1. What are some adjectives you could use to describe the way the mice think and act in this story? Provide at least 4.

2. How does the mice's plan backfire?

3. Which of these words from the second paragraph is an adjective?

   A. Mice
   B. Frequent
   C. Leaders
   D. Exposed

4. How does the story prove the author's point that "The more honor the more danger?"

   A. The mice who were chosen as leaders were the most likely to die
   B. The weasels fought without honor, which allowed them to easily beat the mice
   C. The mice were so obsessed with honoring each other that they never learned how to fight
   D. The mice became too brave, which led to them needing to run away at the end

5. Explain one way the mice could've improved or strengthened their plan to improve the outcome:

⭐ **Directions:**

Circle the **adjectives** in the sentences below. Then, **draw an arrow** from each adjective that points toward the noun it's modifying.

1. My mom's new car is easy to find because the purple paint stands out.

2. The easy way to cross the river is to take the covered bridge.

3. Scrambled eggs are my favorite thing to eat for breakfast.

4. Catherine's younger sister Nicole is an outstanding student.

5. The quick, brown fox jumped over the lazy dog.

FITNESS

Repeat these
**exercises
3 ROUNDS**

Please be aware of your environment and be safe at all times. If you cannot do an exercise, just try your best.

1 - Abs:
3 times

2 - Lunges: 2 times to each leg.
Note: Use your body weight or books as weight to do leg lunges.

3 - Plank: 6 sec.

4 - Run: 50m
Note: Run 25 meters to one side and 25 meters back to the starting position.

Writing a Composition
By James Baldwin

"Children, tomorrow I shall expect all of you to write compositions," said the teacher of Love Lane School. "Then, on Friday those who have done the best may stand up and read their compositions to the school."

Some of the children were pleased, and some were not.

"What shall we write about?" they asked.

"You may choose any subject that you like best," said the teacher.

Some of them thought that "Home" was a good subject. Others liked "School." One little boy chose "The Horse." A little girl said she would write about "Summer."

The next day, every pupil except one had written a composition.

"Henry Longfellow," said the teacher, "why have you not written?"

"Because I don't know how," answered Henry. He was only a child.

"Well," said the teacher, "you can write words, can you not?"

"Yes, sir," said the boy.

"After you have written three or four words, you can put them together, can you not?"

"Yes, sir; I think so."

"Well, then," said the teacher, "you may take your slate and go out behind the schoolhouse for half an hour. Think of something to write about, and write the word on your slate. Then try to tell what it is, what it is like, what it is good for, and what is done with it. That is the way to write a composition."

Henry took his slate and went out. Just behind the schoolhouse was Mr. Finney's barn. Quite close to the barn was a garden. And in the garden, Henry saw a turnip.

"Well, I know what that is," he said to himself; and he wrote the word turnip on his slate. Then he tried to tell what it was like, what it was good for, and what was done with it.

Before the half hour was ended he had written a very neat composition on his slate. He then went into the house, and waited while the teacher read it.

The teacher was surprised and pleased. He said, "Henry Longfellow, you have done very well. Today you may stand up before the school and read what you have written about the turnip."

1. How would you describe Henry Longfellow using adjectives?

2. How is the advice Henry Longfellow's teacher gives him connected to the concept of adjectives?

3. Based on what you read, which of these is the best definition for slate?

   A. A dinnerplate
   B. A pencil
   C. A miniature chalkboard
   D. A kind of turnip

4. Why does young Henry write about the turnip?

   A. Because he loves turnips
   B. Because his family are farmers
   C. Because he doesn't know what else to write about
   D. Because he's never seen a turnip before

5. If you were given the same assignment as Henry Longfellow and his classmates, what topic would you write about in your composition and why?

⭐ **Directions:**

Fill in the blank for each sentence by inserting an **adjective** that makes sense and matches with the **noun** it's describing. The information at the end of the sentence will help you figure out what kind of adjective you need.

1. The _____ robot went out of control and began to attack the city. **(WHAT ADJECTIVE WOULD DESCRIBE A ROBOT LIKE THAT?)**

2. Spending time with your family is a very _____ activity. **(WHAT ADJECTIVE WOULD DESCRIBE THAT EXPERIENCE?)**

3. The _____ puppy ran around the room, chewing its toy. **(WHAT ADJECTIVE WOULD DESCRIBE A PUPPY ACTING LIKE THAT?)**

4. The _____ car broke down in the middle of the intersection. **(WHAT ADJECTIVE WOULD DESCRIBE A CAR THAT WAS ABOUT TO BREAK?)**

5. I never leave the house without my _____ pen. **(WHAT ADJECTIVE WOULD DESCRIBE A PEN YOU WOULDN'T LEAVE HOME WITHOUT?)**

FITNESS

Please be aware of your environment and be safe at all times. If you cannot do an exercise, just try your best.

Repeat these **exercises 3 ROUNDS**

2 - Side Bending: 5 times to each side. Note: try to touch your feet.

3 - Tree Pose: Stay as long as possible. Note: do the same with the other leg.

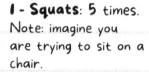

1 - Squats: 5 times. Note: imagine you are trying to sit on a chair.

Mixed Math Questions:

1. Melissa ran 9 miles more than Joe last week. Melissa ran 28 miles. How many miles did Joe run?

   A. 37 miles
   B. 10 miles
   C. 18 miles
   D. 19 miles

2. How old is Vlad if he will be 75 years old in thirteen years?

   A. 88 years old
   B. 62 years old
   C. 71 years old
   D. 49 years old

3. After paying $7 for a sandwich, Jessica has $13. How much money did she have before buying the sandwich?

   A. $27
   B. $18
   C. $20
   D. $6

4. Jessica types 28 words per minute. Mike types 9 words less than Jessica per minute. How many words per minute does Mike type?

   A. 65
   B. 19
   C. 37
   D. 34

5. Bill was 53 years old thirteen years ago. How old is he now?

   A. 63 years old
   B. 79 years old
   C. 66 years old
   D. 40 years old

6. Jose wants to buy a shirt for $64. He gives the cashier $100. How much change does he receive?

   A. $128
   B. $36
   C. $40
   D. $164

7. Lisa wants to buy movie tickets for $159. She gives the cashier $200. What is her change?

   A. $46
   B. $359
   C. $318
   D. $41

8. A recipe for a cupcake calls for 8 cups of flour. Liza has already put in 4 cups. How many more cups does she need to put in?

   A. 2 cups of flour
   B. 1 cup of flour
   C. 4 cups of flour
   D. 3 cups of flour

9. What is the price of one pencil if six pencils cost $12?

   A. $1
   B. $2
   C. $3
   D. $4

10. Matthew will be 20 years old in eight years. How old is he now?

   A. 10 years old
   B. 12 years old
   C. 4 years old
   D. 28 years old

11. How does 11,000 relate to 1,100?

   A. 1,100 is 10 times larger than 11,000.
   B. 11,000 is 10 times smaller than 1,100.
   C. 1,100 is 100 times smaller than 11,000.
   D. 11,000 is 10 times larger than 1,100.

12. Which number is 10 times more than 380?

    A. 38
    B. 3810
    C. 3800
    D. 1038

13. Which number is 10 times less than 240?

    A. 2400
    B. 2410
    C. 250
    D. 24

14. How does 960 compare to 9,600?

    A. It is ten times smaller.
    B. It is ten times larger.
    C. It is ten less.
    D. It is ten more.

15. Which number is the smallest?

    A. three thousand, eight hundred fifty-two
    B. thirty thousand, five hundred eighty-two
    C. thirty-three thousand, eight hundred fifty-two
    D. three thousand, five hundred eighty-two

16. Which sign completes the comparison below?

    70,000 + 8,000 + 900 + 60 + 8 _____
    80,000 + 7, 000 + 600 + 80 +9

    A. >
    B. <
    C. ≥
    D. ≤

17. Which number equals eight hundred thousand, seven hundred twenty-nine?

    A. 872, 900
    B. 800, 709
    C. 807, 029
    D. 800, 729

18. Which sign completes the comparison below?

    850,625 _____ 805, 625

    A. >
    B. <
    C. ≥
    D. ≤

19. Round to the nearest ten-thousand.
    68,352

    A. 60,000
    B. 68,000
    C. 70,000
    D. 7,000

Repeat these exercises **3 ROUNDS**

Please be aware of your environment and be safe at all times. If you cannot do an exercise, just try your best.

1 - Bend forward: 10 times.
Note: try to touch your feet. Make sure to keep your back straight and if needed you can bend your knees.

2 - Lunges: 3 times to each leg.
Note: Use your body weight or books as weight to do leg lunges.

3 - Plank: 6 sec.

4 - Abs:
10 times

Mixed Math Questions:

1. Lara drew 100 greeting cards and handed out 44 to her relatives. For the remaining greeting cards, she wants to hand it out to 8 of her friends evenly (each friend will receive the same number of cards). How many cards will each friend receive?

   A. 5
   B. 7
   C. 9
   D. 11

2. There were 16 necklaces that each had 31 beads. If Shana took all the beads off and put an equal amount on 7 chains, how many beads would be left over?

   A. 0
   B. 2
   C. 4
   D. 6

3. Which number is NOT a factor of 24?

   A. 2
   B. 3
   C. 4
   D. 5

4. Which number below is composite?

   A. 5
   B. 7
   C. 9
   D. 11

5. Which number below is prime?

   A. 25
   B. 53
   C. 70
   D. 99

6. Which number has factors that include both 9 and 3?

   A. 12
   B. 15
   C. 18
   D. 21

7. Haley bought 3 tops that cost $11 each and 2 pairs of jeans that cost $29 each. She gave the cashier $100. How much change should Haley get?

   A. $3
   B. $5
   C. $7
   D. $9

8. Sal came up with a rule of "add 4". Two of his numbers were 43 then 47. What would his next number be?

   A. 39
   B. 49
   C. 51
   D. 55

9. Which set of numbers has the rule "subtract 3"?

   A. 14, 17, 21, 24
   B. 43, 39, 35, 31
   C. 57, 54, 51, 48
   D. 35, 30, 25, 20

10. What rule is shown by the numbers 17, 21, 25, 29?

    A. Add 2
    B. Add 3
    C. Add 4
    D. Add 5

11. Julian bought **72** marbles. If he wants to divide them equally between **8** bags, which equation represent how many marbles will be in each bag?

   A. 72 + 8 = 80
   B. 8 ÷ 72 = 9
   C. 9 ÷ 72 = 8
   D. 72 ÷ 8 = 9

12. Mr. Ellis walked **7** laps this morning and it took him **49** minutes total. If each lap took an equal amount of time to walk, how many minutes did each lap take?

   A. 6 minutes
   B. 7 minutes
   C. 8 minutes
   D. 9 minutes

13. What is the product of 8 and 7?

   A. 15
   B. 63
   C. 64
   D. 56

14. What is the product of 4 x (2 + 7)?

   A. 36
   B. 28
   C. 14
   D. 15

15. Kaylen can either buy **2** packs of markers for **$5** each or **5** packs of pens for **$2** each. Which is going to be more expensive?

   A. The markers will be more expensive, because they are $5
   B. The markers will be more expensive, because 2 x $5 = $10
   C. The pens will be more expensive, because 5 x $2 = $10
   D. The markers and pens will be the same price because 5 x $2 = 2 x $5

16. Jasmine has **4** boxes of crayons. If there are **39** in each box, about how many crayons does she have total?

   A. 43 crayons
   B. 40 crayons
   C. 160 crayons
   D. 150 crayons

FITNESS

Repeat these **exercises 3 ROUNDS**

Please be aware of your environment and be safe at all times. If you cannot do an exercise, just try your best.

1 - High Plank: 6 sec.

2 - Chair: 10 sec. Note: sit on an imaginary chair, keep your back straight.

3 - Waist Hooping: 10 times. Note: if you do not have a hoop, pretend you have an imaginary hoop and rotate your hips 10 times.

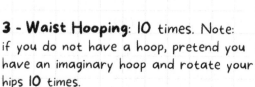

4 - Abs: 10 times

Large Numbers: Addition and
Subtraction Practice

1. 621 - 214

A. 664
B. -343
C. 407
D. -31

2. (-942) - (-419)

A. 165
B. -523
C. -826
D. -46

3. 41 + (-123)

A. -82
B. 834
C. 68
D. 570

4. 71 - (-894)

A. 965
B. 1553
C. 1527
D. 449

5. 125 + (-670)

A. -774
B. -804
C. -1369
D. -545

6. (-524) - 967

A. -2047
B. -1491
C. -2274
D. -1958

7. (-93) + 669

A. 576
B. 872
C. 333
D. 1354

8. (-490) + 179

A. -311
B. 494
C. 388
D. 201

9. (-547) + (-446)

A. -1635
B. -863
C. -1845
D. -993

10. (-764) + 788

A. -507
B. -837
C. -847
D. 24

11. (-932) + 877

A. 197
B. -1030
C. -55
D. 328

12. (-801) - (-259)

A. -542
B. -810
C. -846
D. -1317

13. (-535) + (-635)

A. -1935
B. -1402
C. -1170
D. -983

14. (-110) + (-620)

 A. -1118
 B. 170
 C. -730
 D. -1565

15. 711 - 287

 A. 69
 B. 481
 C. 115
 D. 424

16. (-155) - (-398)

 A. 393
 B. -292
 C. 1067
 D. 243

17. 422 - (-672)

 A. 1094
 B. 1781
 C. 366
 D. 1215

18. (-439) - (-607)

 A. -122
 B. 168
 C. 131
 D. -690

19. (-132) + (-26)

 A. -158
 B. -804
 C. -50
 D. 699

20. 525 - 844

 A. -413
 B. 124
 C. -319
 D. -1054

YOGA

Please be aware of your environment and be safe at all times. If you cannot do an exercise, just try your best.

1 - Down Dog: 10 sec.

2 - Bend Down: 10 sec.

3 - Chair: 10 sec.

4 - Child Pose: 20 sec.

5 - Shavasana: as long as you can. Note: think of happy moments and relax your mind.

WEEK 11 DAY 6 🐟 EXPERIMENT

Collecting and Graphing Outdoor Temperature Data

The weather is a favorite topic of discussion for many people. In order to build a basic understanding of both weather and climate, you need to be able to **measure temperatures** and **notice trends**.

Materials:

- One outdoor thermometer (it can be a traditional mercury thermometer or a modern, digital one - all that matters is that it's designed to measure outdoor temperatures and can be kept in the same place for a week)
- Graph paper
- Notepaper
- A ruler
- Art supplies (crayons, colored pencils, markers, etc.)

Procedure:

1. Make sure your **outdoor thermometer is secured** in a place where it can safely sit for a week. Unlike our past experiments, we'll be doing this one in the background for several days.

2. Commit to a time that you will **consistently check the thermometer each day** between now and next Friday (it could be 8AM or noon or 3PM or anytime you want - it's just consistency that's important).

3. Beginning today, check the temperature on the outdoor thermometer at the same time each day and **record it on your note sheet**. You can also take some notes about other aspects of the weather you observe: Is it raining? Windy? Humid?

4. At the end of your test period (next Friday) review your notes and answer the two Follow-Up Questions below.

5. Then, using your notes, graph paper, ruler, and art supplies, create a **bar graph** that shows the fluctuations in temperature from day-to-day throughout the week. Be sure to label each bar as one day of the week and use the height of the bars to communicate temperature.

WEEK 11 DAY 6  EXPERIMENT

Follow-Up Questions:

1. During the time you conducted your experiment, **how much did the temperature change from day to day?**

~~~~~~

~~~~~~

~~~~~~

2. Did you observe any connections or **relationships between the temperature and other aspects of the weather** (for example, was it colder on days it rained)?

~~~~~~

~~~~~~

~~~~~~

YOGA

Please be aware of your environment and be safe at all times. If you cannot do an exercise, just try your best.

1 - Tree Pose: Stay as long as possible. Note: do on one leg then on another.

2 - Down Dog: 10 sec.

3 - Stretching: Stay as long as possible. Note: do on one leg then on another.

4 - Lower Plank: 6 sec. Note: Keep your back straight and body tight.

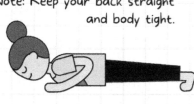

5 - Book Pose: 6 sec. Note: Keep your core tight. Legs should be across from your eyes.

6 - Shavasana: 5 min. Note: this pose is very important and provides you with long term benefits. Try not to skip this. Close your eyes and imagine who you want to be and what your goals are! Always think happy thoughts.

Task: Which of these bugs crawl along the same side of the grass leaf as bug 1 does?

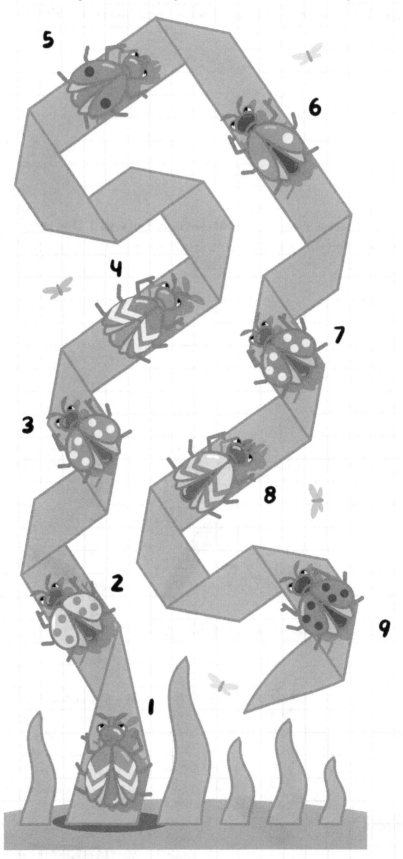

You are a superstar!
This is your last week in the workbook. You are ready to conquer 4th grade!

WEEK 12

It's a lobster!

Did you know that lobsters can live as long as 100 years? They have an exoskeleton which protects them. Lobsters go through molting to grow where they must shed their exoskeleton.

ARGOPREP

Last week, we looked at how **adjectives** make sentences more interesting by describing **nouns**. We can also improve our sentences by adding some more detail to our **verbs** and **adjectives**. Special words called **adverbs** are used to give us more information about the action of a sentence.

 Key Terms

Adverb: A word that is used to describe or modify a verb or adjective
Verb: A word that describes an action or a state something is in
Adjective: A word that describes or modifies a noun

For Example...

Adverbs can provide us with lots of different information about the verbs they modify. An adverb can tell us **how** something happened, **when** something happened, **where** something happened, **how often** something happens, and more!

An adverb can also be used to "pump up" or provide even more information about an adjective (Instead of just saying something is **big**, you can say it is **really big!**).

HINT: A lot of the time (but not always), adverbs end in -ly

Examples of Adverbs		
Quickly	Before	Really
Regularly	Explosively	Sadly
Slowly	Very	Always
Soon	Sometimes	Happily

In the sentence:

◉ Mike runs <u>quickly</u>.
   🐚 **Quickly** is an adverb that modifies the verb **runs**
      🔵 It tells you **how** Mike runs

◉ Mike is <u>incredibly</u> quick when he runs.
   🐚 **Incredibly** is an adverb that modifies the adjective **quick**
      🔵 It tells you **how quick** Mike is

◉ I was <u>very</u> happy to learn that you <u>always</u> wash your hands before you eat.
   🐚 **Very** is an adverb that modifies the adjective **happy**
      🔵 It tells you **how happy** the speaker is
   🐚 **Always** is an adverb that modifies the verb **wash**
      🔵 It tells you **how often** the person washes their hands

The Man, the Horse, the Ox, and the Dog
By Aesop

A Horse, Ox, and Dog, driven to great straits by the cold, sought shelter and protection from Man. He received them kindly, lighted a fire, and warmed them.

He let the Horse make free with his oats, gave the Ox an abundance of hay, and fed the Dog with meat from his own table. Grateful for these favors, the animals determined to repay him to the best of their ability. For this purpose, they divided the term of his life between them, and each endowed one portion of it with the qualities which chiefly characterized himself.

The Horse chose his earliest years and gave them his own attributes: hence every man is in his youth impetuous, headstrong, and obstinate in maintaining his own opinion.

The Ox took under his patronage the next term of life, and therefore man in his middle age is fond of work, devoted to labor, and resolute to amass wealth and to husband his resources.

The end of life was reserved for the Dog, wherefore the old man is often snappish, irritable, hard to please, and selfish, tolerant only of his own household, but averse to strangers and to all who do not administer to his comfort or to his necessities.

1. Why are the animals grateful to the man in the story?

2. How are the qualities of the Ox different from those of the Horse or the Dog?

3. Which of these words from the second paragraph is an adverb?

    A. Abundance
    B. Grateful
    C. Qualities
    D. Chiefly

4. Based on the story, which of these statements is **not** true about the Dog's personality?

    A. Dogs are loyal to their friends and families
    B. Dogs are distrustful of strangers
    C. Dogs work hard for their loved ones
    D. Dogs are hard to please

5. What aspect of life is this story trying to explain? What could this be a metaphor for?

⭐ **Directions:**

Circle the **adverbs** in the sentences below. There may be more than one adverb per sentence!

1. That oil painting of my mother is very old.

2. The eagle flew swiftly from tree to tree.

3. I never forget my watch because I always put it near my car keys.

4. My hair got extremely wet when Wade dumped that freezing cold bucket of water on me.

5. I rarely eat beef, but when I do, it's usually a cheeseburger.

Repeat these **exercises 3 ROUNDS**

Please be aware of your environment and be safe at all times. If you cannot do an exercise, just try your best.

1 - Abs: 3 times

2 - Lunges: 2 times to each leg. Note: Use your body weight or books as weight to do leg lunges.

3 - Plank: 6 sec.

4 - Run: 50m Note: Run 25 meters to one side and 25 meters back to the starting position.

The Shepherd-Boy Painter
By James Baldwin

One day a traveler was walking through a part of Italy where a great many sheep were pasturing. Near the top of a hill he saw a little shepherd boy who was lying on the ground while a flock of sheep and lambs were grazing around him.

As he came nearer he saw that the boy held a charred stick in his hand, with which he was drawing something on a flat rock. The lad was so much interested in his work that he did not see the stranger.

The stranger bent over him and looked at the picture he had made on the rock. It was the picture of a sheep, and it was drawn so well that the stranger was filled with astonishment.

"What is your name, my boy?" he said.

The lad was startled. He jumped to his feet and looked up at the kind gentleman.

"My name is Giotto," he answered.

"What is your father's name?"

"Bondone."

"And whose sheep are these?"

"They belong to the rich man who lives in the big white house there among the trees. My father works in the field, and I take care of the sheep."

"How would you like to live with me, Giotto? I would teach you how to draw pictures of sheep and horses, and even of men," said the stranger. The boy's face beamed with delight.

"I should like to learn to do that - oh, ever so much!" he answered. "But I must do as father says.""Let us go and ask him," said the stranger.

The stranger's name was Cimabue. He was the most famous painter of the time. His pictures were known and admired in every city of Italy.

Bondone was surprised when Cimabue offered to take his little boy to

Florence and teach him to be a great painter.

"I know that the lad can draw pictures wonderfully well," he said. "He does not like to do anything else. Perhaps he will do well with you. Yes, you may take him."

In the city of Florence little Giotto saw some of the finest pictures in the world. He learned so fast that he could soon paint as well as Cimabue himself.

1. How would you describe the character of Cimabue?

2. What are two reasons Bondone allows Giotto to go with Cimabue?

3. Which of these objects is the closest thing to the "charred stick" that Giotto uses in the second paragraph?

    A. A ruler
    B. A pencil
    C. A sword
    D. A flashlight

4. Which of these words from the first paragraph of the story is an adverb?

    A. Walking
    B. Great
    C. Top
    D. Grazing

5. Write a three-sentence description of Giotto's picture of the sheep (from the second and third paragraphs). Use at least three adjectives and at least three adverbs:

⭐ **Directions:**

Circle the **adverbs** in the sentences below. Then, **draw an arrow** from each adverb that points toward the verb or adjective it's modifying. There may be more than one adverb per sentence!

1. I definitely think we took a wrong turn back there.

2. It's really smart to save your money responsibly, rather than spending it.

3. The sun rises in the east daily and sets in the west nightly.

4. That movie was pretty scary, even though the special effects looked really fake.

5. The children laughed happily as the clown slipped dramatically and fell.

FITNESS

Please be aware of your environment and be safe at all times. If you cannot do an exercise, just try your best.

Repeat these **exercises 3 ROUNDS**

3 - Side Bending: 5 times to each side. Note: try to touch your feet.

4 - Abs: 10 times

2 - Squats: 5 times. Note: imagine you are trying to sit on a chair.

5 - Tree Pose: Stay as long as possible. Note: do the same with the other leg.

1 - High Plank: 6 sec.

Mixed Problems

1. $\frac{7}{15}$ ----- $\frac{14}{30}$

   A. >
   B. <
   C. =
   D. ≥

2. $\frac{6}{10} + \frac{2}{10} =$

   A. $\frac{4}{10}$
   B. $\frac{8}{10}$
   C. $\frac{10}{10}$
   D. $\frac{8}{20}$

3. Jacey has a goal to work out 6 hours a week. She rides her bike for $\frac{1}{2}$ hour for three days and walks with her mom for 1 hour another day. How many more hours does she need to exercise to reach her goal?

   A. $2\frac{1}{2}$ hours
   B. 3 hours
   C. $3\frac{1}{2}$ hours
   D. 4 hours

4. Write the equivalent fraction for the number 0.53.

   A. $\frac{1}{53}$
   B. $\frac{53}{100}$
   C. $\frac{53}{10}$
   D. $\frac{5}{10}$

5. Which sign completes the comparison?

   0.86 ____ 0.68

   Answer _____

6. 364 ÷ 7 =

   A. 50
   B. 52
   C. 62
   D. 71

7. 13,972 + 7,283

   A. 22,155
   B. 21,255
   C. 25,215
   D. 22,125

8. 42568 - 423

   A. 42,415
   B. 45,215
   C. 42,145
   D. 41,245

9. Which answer choice is equal to 8 hours?

   A. 48 minutes
   B. 480 minutes
   C. 4.8 minutes
   D. 64 minutes

10. The perimeter of a garden measures 66 feet. If the width is 11 feet, what is the length?

   A. 22 ft
   B. 11 ft
   C. 44 feet
   D. 10 feet

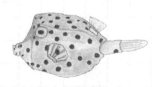

11. The Smith family is taking a ten hour road trip. They brought 4 movies to watch on the trip. Two movies are 2 hours long, one movie is 2 hours 15 minutes and one movie is 1 hour 55 minutes. How much time will they have left on the road trip after watching all four movies?

A. 1 hour
B. 1 hour 50 mins
C. 8 hours 50 mins
D. 8 hours

12. The length of Eric's bedroom is 12 feet and 9 inches. The width of the room is 2 feet and 8 inches less than the length. What is the width of Eric's bedroom?

A. 10 feet, 1 inch
B. 10 feet
C. 10 feet, 5 inches
D. 10 feet, 2 inches

13. Emily and Christopher and running a relay race. Christopher completed the race in 32 minutes. Emily took 9 minutes longer to complete the race. How long did it take them to run the race in all?

A. 41 minutes
B. 50 minutes
C. 1 hour 13 minutes
D. 1 hour 3 minutes

14. Amanda spent 45 minutes exercising last week. Missy spent double the amount of time exercising. How much time did Missy spend exercising?

A. 1 hour
B. 1 hour 30 minutes
C. 2 hours
D. 45 minutes

15. Using the line plot below, where would you graph $9\frac{3}{4}$?

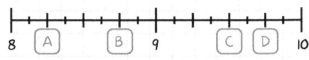

A. Point A
B. Point B
C. Point C
D. Point D

FITNESS

Repeat these
exercises
3 ROUNDS

Please be aware of your environment and be safe at all times. If you cannot do an exercise, just try your best.

1 - Bend forward: 10 times.
Note: try to touch your feet. Make sure to keep your back straight and if needed you can bend your knees.

2 - Lunges: 3 times to each leg.
Note: Use your body weight or books as weight to do leg lunges.

3 - Plank: 6 sec.

4 - Abs:
10 times

Mixed Problems

1. Which shape contains only 1 set of parallel lines?

   A. Trapezoid
   B. Triangle
   C. Circle
   D. Pentagon

2. Which shape does not contain 2 sets of perpendicular lines?

   A. Rectangle
   B. Square
   C. Diamond
   D. Triangle

3. Which shape does not contain parallel or perpendicular lines?

   A. Trapezoid
   B. Circle
   C. Rectangle
   D. Rhombus

4. Which angle measurement would define a triangle as an obtuse triangle?

   A. 90°
   B. 24°
   C. 110°
   D. 72°

5. Jason needs $20 to get a new radio. He has $5 already. If he gets $5 allowance each week, how many more weeks will he need to save his allowance to afford the radio?

   A. 3 weeks
   B. 4 weeks
   C. 5 weeks
   D. 6 weeks

6. Ashley has 123 beads. Sheldon has twice as many beads as Ashley. How many beads do they have altogether?

   A. 246 beads
   B. 245 beads
   C. 368 beads
   D. 369 beads

7. Which pattern can be described by "multiples of 4"?

   A. 4, 8, 12, 15, 19
   B. 4, 8, 10, 14, 18
   C. 4, 8, 12, 16, 22
   D. 4, 8, 12, 16, 20

8. Which of the following situations represents "half"?

   A. Two friends each have 1 cookie
   B. Two friends each have 2 cookies
   C. Three friends equally sharing 1 cookie
   D. Two friends equally sharing 1 cookie

9. Kady made 5 cakes. Each cake was divided equally into 12 pieces. How many pieces of cake does Kady have altogether?

   A. 65 pieces
   B. 60 pieces
   C. 55 pieces
   D. 50 pieces

10. Jamill made a cake. He cut it into 8 equal slices. He has not eaten any of the cake. Which fraction does not represent how much cake Jamill has left?

    A. $\frac{1}{8}$
    B. eight-eighths
    C. one whole
    D. $\frac{8}{8}$

11. Jim is going to the movies in **2** hours. It is now **4:45pm**. What time is Jim going to the movies?

    A. 2:45pm
    B. 4:47pm
    C. 6:45pm
    D. 6:47pm

12. Mr. Hill is going to ring the bell at a quarter till four in the afternoon. What time will he ring the bell?

    A. 4:15pm
    B. 3:45pm
    C. 4:15am
    D. 3:45am

13. Mrs. Hernandez needs to meet her daughter at the airport at **6:00pm**. It takes **50** minutes to drive to the airport. What time should Mrs. Hernandez leave for the airport?

    A. 6:50pm
    B. 6:10pm
    C. 5:10pm
    D. 5:50pm

14. A biologist wants to weigh a feather that he found. Which would be the best estimate of the feather?

    A. 20 grams
    B. 20,000 grams
    C. 20 kilograms
    D. 2 kilograms

15. Which of the following would be the best estimate when measuring a small cup of milk?

    A. 40 kilograms
    B. 4,000 grams
    C. 40 liters
    D. 400 milliliters

16. The pet store owner has a bucket that holds **5** liters. If he wants to fill up a **25** liter fish tank, how many times will he have to fill up the bucket?

    A. 7 times
    B. 6 times
    C. 5 times
    D. 4 times

FITNESS

Please be aware of your environment and be safe at all times. If you cannot do an exercise, just try your best.

Repeat these **exercises 3 ROUNDS**

2 - High Plank: 6 sec.

1 - Waist Hooping: 10 times. Note: if you do not have a hoop, pretend you have an imaginary hoop and rotate your hips 10 times.

3 - Chair: 10 sec.
Note: sit on an imaginary chair, keep your back straight.

4 - Abs: 10 times

Mixed Problems

Use the diagram below to answer questions 1 - 5.

Favorite Shapes in our classroom

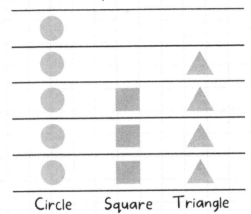

Circle   Square   Triangle

Key: Each shape is equal to 2 votes

1. What type of data was collected to create this pictograph?

    A. Number of students in the classroom
    B. Number of shapes in the classroom
    C. Which shapes are the favorite in the classroom
    D. Which students are the favorite in the classroom

2. Which shape is the most popular in the classroom?

    A. Circle
    B. Square
    C. Triangle
    D. They are all equal

3. Based on the key, how many total students were asked what their favorite shape is?

    A. 12
    B. 18
    C. 24
    D. 26

4. How many more students liked circles than squares?

    A. 2 students
    B. 3 students
    C. 4 students
    D. 5 students

5. What would be another good title for this pictograph?

    A. Types of Shapes
    B. Colors of Shapes
    C. Shapes We Like
    D. Counting Shapes

Adding and Subtracting Decimals

1. 394 + 418.8

    A. 1060.6
    B. 1214.9
    C. 596.7
    D. 812.8

2. 172.4 - 94.7

    A. 525.6
    B. 491.3
    C. 152.8
    D. 77.7

3. 389.9 - 39.4

    A. 578.7
    B. 245.3
    C. 350.5
    D. 30.2

4. 154.7 + 432.3

    A. 587
    B. 810.8
    C. 676.3
    D. 495.3

5. 317.88 - 11.4

    A. 516.48
    B. 293.11
    C. 429.58
    D. 306.48

6. 277.7 - 98.3

    A. 189.5
    B. 15.4
    C. 81.7
    D. 179.4

7. 323.6 + 49.01

    A. 500.11
    B. 50.21
    C. 372.61
    D. 739.81

8. 460 - 305.61

    A. 161.39
    B. 154.39
    C. 95.49
    D. 113.79

9. 498.5 + 66.6

    A. 557.62
    B. 565.1
    C. 1002.7
    D. 939.9

10. 341.4 - 292.31

    A. 13.19
    B. 49.09
    C. 395.69
    D. 543.59

Multiplication Drills:

11. 13 × 5

    A. 80
    B. 54
    C. 18
    D. 65

12. 7 × 8

    A. 50
    B. 15
    C. 32
    D. 56

YOGA

Please be aware of your environment and be safe at all times. If you cannot do an exercise, just try your best.

1 - Down Dog: 10 sec.

2 - Bend Down: 10 sec.

3 - Chair: 10 sec.

4 - Child Pose: 20 sec.

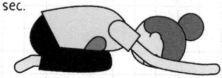

5 - Shavasana: as long as you can. Note: think of happy moments and relax your mind.

WEEK 12 DAY 6  EXPERIMENT

Collecting and Graphing Indoor Temperature Data

Last week, you conducted a study of **outdoor** temperatures. This week, we'll move our experiment **indoors** to see how (and if) temperature fluctuates inside your house.

Materials:

- One indoor thermometer (it can be a traditional mercury thermometer or a modern, digital one - all that matters is that it's designed to measure outdoor temperatures and can be kept in the same place for a week)
- Graph paper
- Notepaper
- A ruler
- Art supplies (crayons, colored pencils, markers, etc.)

Procedure:

1. Make sure your **indoor thermometer is secured** in a place where it can safely sit for a week. Unlike our past experiments, we'll be doing this one in the background for several days.

2. Commit to a time that you will **consistently check the thermometer each day** between now and next Friday (it could be 8AM or noon or 3PM or anytime you want - it's just consistency that's important).

3. Beginning today, check the temperature on the indoor thermometer at the same time each day and **record it on your note sheet**. You can also take some notes about other aspects of the indoor environment you notice: is there an air conditioning unit or heater running? Is there a fan in the room? Are there a large number of people gathered in the room?

4. At the end of your test period (next Friday) review your notes and answer the two Follow-Up Questions below.

5. Then, using your notes, graph paper, ruler, and art supplies, create a **bar graph** that shows the fluctuations in temperature from day-to-day throughout the week. Be sure to label each bar as one day of the week and use the height of the bars to communicate temperature.

Follow-Up Questions:

1. Comparing your data to what you observed last week, does the temperature tend to fluctuate more **indoors or outside**? How did you get your answer?

~~~~~~

~~~~~~

~~~~~~

2. Did you observe any connections or **relationships between the temperature and other aspects of the indoor environment** (for example, was it hotter on days when more people were hanging out in the room)?

~~~~~~

~~~~~~

~~~~~~

YOGA

Please be aware of your environment and be safe at all times. If you cannot do an exercise, just try your best.

1 - Tree Pose: Stay as long as possible. Note: do on one leg then on another.

2 - Down Dog: 10 sec.

3 - Stretching: Stay as long as possible. Note: do on one leg then on another.

4 - Lower Plank: 6 sec. Note: Keep your back straight and body tight.

5 - Book Pose: 6 sec. Note: Keep your core tight. Legs should be across from your eyes.

6 - Shavasana: 5 min. Note: this pose is very important and provides you with long term benefits. Try not to skip this. Close your eyes and imagine who you want to be and what your goals are! Always think happy thoughts.

226

ANSWER
SHEET

ARGOPREP

ANSWER SHEET

WEEK 1 DAY 1

Reading Comprehension:

1. The Hare is trying to escape being caught/killed by a pack of hounds

2. The other animals claimed to be the hare's friends, but their actions demonstrated that they were not friends at all.

3. C - In paragraph 3, it clearly states, "The goat, however, feared that his back might do her some harm..."

4. D - "Unable" contains the prefix "un." None of the other phrases contain words with prefixes.

5. Answers will slightly vary. The hare thought she had many different friends, but it actually turned out that she had no true friends.

English/Grammar Activity:

1. Untrained should be circled. It means "not trained."

2. Misaligned should be circled. It means "Aligned incorrectly."

3. Retake should be circled. It means "Take again."

4. Autocorrect should be circled. It means "Self-correcting."

5. Refresh should be circled. It means "To load up again."

WEEK 1 DAY 2

Reading Comprehension:

1. The other characters pay no attention to the little bird, but Lincoln wants to help it.

2. B - The other men are unhelpful because they do not provide the bird with help.

3. Lincoln has to climb the tree to put the bird back in his nest, which shows his willingness to go out of his way to help.

4. The text states the lawyers "thought it so foolish that a strong man should take so much trouble just for some worthless young birds."

5. Answers will vary. The author puts a great deal of effort into describing Lincoln's desire to help others and also wraps the passage up by briefly discussing how Lincoln was a very important person.

English/Grammar Activity:

1. Reapply

2. Autopilot

3. Untrustworthy

4. Transcribe

5. Anti-stress

ANSWER SHEET

WEEK 1 / DAY 3

Addition Practice
Questions

1. B
2. A
3. 690
4. 614
5. B
6. C
7. 853
8. 1,106
9. D
10. B

Subtraction Practice
Questions

1. B
2. 552
3. 483
4. A
5. 475
6. B
7. C
8. B
9. 272
10. 660

WEEK 1 / DAY 4

Multiplication Practice
Questions

1. A
2. C
3. B
4. B
5. C
6. 4 x 15 or 15 x 4
7. 4
8. B
9. 104
10. 630

Division Practice
Questions

1. B

WEEK 1 / DAY 5

Division Practice
Questions

1. C
2. 80
3. 11
4. A
5. C
6. 9
7. 4
8. 120
9. 90

Word problems: add/
subtract/multiply/divide

1. B
2. C
3. A
4. C
5. B
6. 52
7. 4 months
8. 6 pencils
9. 283
10. 912

WEEK 1 / DAY 6

Answers will vary.

ANSWER SHEET

WEEK 2 · DAY 1

Reading Comprehension:

1. In the second paragraph, the Town Mouse explains that he prefers city life because it is easier to find food there than in the country.

2. The Town Mouse focuses on the variety of food available, but the Country Mouse only sees the danger involved in getting it.

3. D - Freedom is the only word that contains a suffix.

4. C - The verb "build" is transformed into the object "building" by attaching -ing.

5. Answers will vary. Some students may say the Town Mouse is more closed-minded because he does not like having to work hard for his food like the Country Mouse. Some students may say the Country Mouse is more closed-minded because he doesn't accept the risks of the city.

English/Grammar Activity:

1. Cheerful should be circled. It means "Full of cheer or happiness."

2. Thoughtless should be circled. It means "Without thought."

3. Player should be circled. It means "Someone who plays something."

4. Edible should be circled. It means "Able to be eaten."

5. Rocking should be circled. It means "Moving around and enjoying music."

WEEK 2 · DAY 2

Reading Comprehension:

1. Benjamin Franklin's family is poor and they have many children.

2. Answers may vary. Generally, though, the boy who sells the whistle is dishonest, a liar, etc.

3. B - He had no pennies, so he was penniless.

4. D Franklin s brother mocks Benjamin for overpaying after he examines the whistle.

5. According to the text, the whistle is only worth one penny, but Franklin paid several pennies for it.

English/Grammar Activity:

1. Joyful

2. Hinduism

3. Stardom

4. Addressee

5. Winless

WEEK 2 🐋 DAY 3

Diagrams:
add/subtract/multiply/
divide

1. B
2. D
3. C
4. B
5. C
6. 410
7. B
8. A
9. C
10. C

WEEK 2 🐋 DAY 4

Diagrams: add/sub-
tract/multiply/divide

1. 32
2. C
3. B

4. 760
5. A
6. B
7. 490
8. A
9. D
10. D

WEEK 2 🐋 DAY 5

Place Value

1. 3
2. hundreds
3. one hundred
4. three
5. D
6. D
7. A
8. C
9. 3
10. B

Standard form vs
expanded form

1. B
2. C
3. D
4. B
5. A
6. 3,622
7. eight thousand five
hundred and sixty-three
8. 7,354
9. 2,000 + 700 + 30 + 9
10. 4,586

WEEK 2 🐋 DAY 6

Answers will vary.

ANSWER SHEET

WEEK 3 — DAY 1

Reading Comprehension:

1. Based on the passage, a miser is someone who is obsessed with money. They prefer to save money rather than spend it.
2. The gold was of no value because the miser was never going to use it. Therefore, it was just a pile of stuff buried underground.
3. A - The fact that the town is expanding and new buildings are being build communicates that "Outskirts" means the outer edges of the town.
4. C - The workers only got interested in the gold because they observed the miser visiting it.
5. Answers will vary. Students will probably say something about consolidating all the wealth into one, easy-to-bury item.

English/Grammar Activity:

1. Magic tricks. Magician, card tricks, and rabbit out of a hat should have been clues.
2. A large gathering. Teachers, students, and assembly hall should have been hints.
3. A prize or form of recognition. Awarded, bravery, and "highest" should all have been hints.
4. Not showing emotion. Held back tears and even though his knee was hurting should have been hints.
5. Boredom. Students, hour left in school, and the fact that they can only read silently or do math should all have been hints.

WEEK 3 — DAY 2

Reading Comprehension:

1. Answers will vary. Book, cover, pictures, words, and school are all examples of good answers.
2. The other characters are happy to see the minister. Also, everybody is careful to treat him with respect by bowing, curtseying, and shaking his hand.
3. C - The fact that "bow" and "curtsey" are so close together in the text should hint they have similar meanings.
4. A - At the beginning of the story, it says that Edward "could read quite well."
5. Based on the story, "to speak a piece," is to give a short speech or read a passage in front of the class.

English/Grammar Activity:

1. **Prefix:** Non
   Root: Refund
   Suffix: Able
   Meaning: Not able to get your money back in exchange for.

2. **Prefix:** Auto
Root: Mobile
Meaning: A machine that moves by itself.

3. **Root:** Appoint
Suffix: -ee
Meaning: Someone put in a certain job by someone else.

4. **Prefix:** Post
Root: Harvest
Meaning: After the harvest

5. **Prefix:** Anti
Root: Consumer
Suffix: Ism
Meaning: Against the idea that people should buy or use lots of things.

WEEK 3 — DAY 3

Rounding to nearest 10, 100 and 1,000

1. D
2. B
3. C
4. A
5. C
6. 670
7. 2,000
8. to the nearest hundred
9. 840 > 830
10. 4,000

Fraction Comparison Problems

1. C
2. C
3. A
4. C
5. B

WEEK 3 — DAY 4

Fraction Comparison Problems

1. $\frac{1}{3} < \frac{2}{4}$
2. (number line: $\frac{4}{10}$, $\frac{1}{2}$, $\frac{3}{5}$ between 0 and 1)
3. 1
4. B
5. $\frac{5}{6} > \frac{2}{3}$

Fractions with diagrams

1. C
2. D
3. B
4. C
5. D
6. $\frac{3}{12} = \frac{1}{4}$
7. $\frac{2}{5}$
8. $\frac{4}{14}$

WEEK 3 — DAY 5

Problems with fractions with diagrams

1. $\frac{1}{8}, \frac{4}{8}, \frac{6}{8}$
2. $\frac{6}{15} = \frac{2}{5}$

Problems with fractions add/subtract and multiply (Same denominator)

1. C
2. B
3. A
4. C
5. D
6. B
7. $\frac{6}{10} - \frac{4}{10} = \frac{2}{10}$
8. $\frac{1}{8} \times 5$
9. $\frac{6}{7}$
10. $\frac{8}{9}$

WEEK 3 — DAY 6

Answers will vary.

ANSWER SHEET

WEEK 4 🐟 DAY 1

Reading Comprehension:

1. The fox is running for its life to escape a pack of hunting dogs.

2. Answers will vary. Generally, the story shows that you shouldn't trust someone just because they promise to help you.

3. C - This is the only sentence that correctly uses "its" as the possessive form of "it."

4. C - This is the only sentence that correctly uses "there" to refer to a place or location.

5. Answers will vary. Students will most likely pick the woodsman because he explicitly lies to the fox.

English/Grammar Activity:

1. Incorrect - "their" should be changed to "they're"

2. Incorrect - "it's" should be changed to "its"

3. Correct

4. Incorrect - "hole" should be corrected to "whole"

5. Incorrect - "too" should be corrected to "two"

WEEK 4 🐟 DAY 2

Reading Comprehension:

1. Answers will vary. James Hogg wants to be a good shepherd, even though he has some challenges. He does not want to fail.

2. The narrator is trying to show that Sirrah is a very special dog and that no human shepherd could have done as well as he did.

3. B - Only B correctly uses "to" to communicate something being given/received.

4. D - Only Answer D correctly uses "there was" to communicate the idea that something exists, as was done in the original sentence from the passage.

5. Answers will vary. Students might point out that Sirrah the dog did all the actual work or argue that James Hogg is the main character because more words are devoted to describing his thoughts and feelings throughout the story.

English/Grammar Activity:

1. There

2. Hole

3. To

4. Its

5. Its

WEEK 4 DAY 3

Shading in fraction models

1. B
2. $\frac{1}{8} + \frac{1}{8} + \frac{1}{8} + \frac{1}{8} + \frac{1}{8} + \frac{1}{8}$

   or $\frac{1}{8} \times 6$
3. $\frac{3}{5}$
4. A
5. $\frac{7}{30}$

Comparing numbers using comparison symbol (<, >, =)

1. A
2. 984 > 976
3. C
4. 564 - 176 > 348
5. A
6. B
7. 869 < 894
8. C
9. 1,329 > 1,316
10. 456 + 138 = 256 + 338

WEEK 4 DAY 4

Area and perimeter

1. B
2. A
3. 17 yd
4. 64 in
5. 13 yd
6. C
7. B
8. D
9. C
10. B

Identifying number patterns

1. 3, 6, **9**, 12, **15**, 18
2. D
3. C

WEEK 4 DAY 5

Identifying number patterns

1. A. "Add 4"

   B. Any shape that has 16 circles is fine;

   One example:

2. A
3. B
4. 10, **22**, 34, 46, **58**, 70
5. "Add 15"
6. D
7. 12, **17**, **22**, 27, **32**, 37

Tables/Charts and understanding data

1. 16 sandwiches
2. A
3. A
4. 3
5. B
6. C

WEEK 4 DAY 6

Answers will vary.

ANSWER SHEET

WEEK 5 DAY 1

Reading Comprehension:

1. Answers will vary. Generally, students will probably say that the donkey was lazy and didn't want to do work. On the other hand, students could also say that the donkey was cautious and didn't want to be overburdened.

2. The first time, the merchant believes the donkey stumbled on accident and simply went back to get more salt. The second time, he understood that the donkey fell on purpose and decided to punish it.

3. C - The phrase "on purpose" shows that the fall was not an accident.

4. C - We know the merchant is already very rich because he can afford so much salt, which the passage explains is very valuable/expensive.

5. Answers will vary. Students might suggest using multiple donkeys, making multiple trips, etc.

English/Grammar Activity:

1. The second sentence should be circled. The words "might be" and "trying out" should have been important hints from the first sentence. The words "probably" and "because she's the best" should have been important hints from the second sentence.

2. The second sentence should be circled. The words "hoping to" and "setting some traps" should have been important hints from the first sentence. The words "calling an exterminator" and "it should be over soon" should have been important hints from the second sentence.

3. The first sentence should be circled. The word "definitely" should have been an important hint from the first sentence. The words "highly likely" should have been important hints from the second sentence.

4. The first sentence should be circled. The words "assume" and "because I know his parents and brother have been there" should have been important hints from the first sentence. The words "I think" and "it's possible" should have been important hints from the second sentence.

5. The first sentence should be circled. The words "must be" should have been important hints from the first sentence. The words "I believe" should have been important hints from the second sentence.

WEEK 5 DAY 2

Reading Comprehension:

1. The two artists are using the certainty of the birds (that the fruit and boy are real) to judge who is the best artist.

2. Zeuxis is proud and highly confident. Parrhasius is just as skilled, but he is curious to test his ability, rather than being certain of it.

3. A - Zeuxis is completely certain in his abilities. We know this because of the line "I am the only man in the world who can paint a picture so true to life."

4. D - We know Parrhasius is uncertain because he only says, "I will see what I can do."

5. Because he was so confident he would win the competition due to his superior abilities, Zeuxis wound up disappointed at the end of the story because he realized he was not as good as the thought he was.

English/Grammar Activity:

1. Hopefully
2. Maybe
3. Could
4. Probably
5. Definitely

WEEK 5 — DAY 3

Tables/Charts and understanding data

1. B
2. D
3. C
4. A

Bar graph & Line graph

1. D
2. Camping
3. C
4. B

WEEK 5 — DAY 4

Bar graph & Line graph

1. A
2. C
3. C
4. B
5. D
6. 3

WEEK 5 — DAY 5

Line of symmetry

1. C
2. C

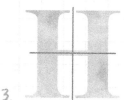

3.
4. B
5. Yes, it is
6. C

7.
8. C
9. B
10. 8

WEEK 5 — DAY 6

Answers will vary.

WEEK 6 ⟩ DAY 1

Reading Comprehension:

1. The original plan was for the thief to check into the hotel without any money and then steal something valuable enough to pay for the room before he checked out.

2. Instead of paying for the room by stealing something as planned, the thief gets the room for free by pretending to be a werewolf.

3. A - "Howl like a wolf" is a simile because it is a comparison that uses "like."

4. C - "Talked the innkeeper's ear off" is an example of figurative language because the innkeeper's ear never literally fell off; it's just a figure of speech. None of the other choices contain examples of figurative language.

5. Answers will vary. Students might suggest the thief trying to work off his debt or just being honest and asking for mercy.

English/Grammar Activity:

1. "The crummiest day of the whole year" should be underlined. It is an example of hyperbole because it is an example of an exaggeration.

2. "Our dog is a monster" should be underlined. It is an example of a metaphor because it compares two things (a dog and a monster) without using "like" or "as."

3. "My smart phone is my best friend" should be underlined. It is an example of personification because it treats an inanimate object (the phone) like a human being (a friend).

4. "I felt like an egg frying in a pan" should be underlined. It is an example of a simile because it compares two things (feeling hot and a frying egg) using the word "like."

5. "The strictest principal in the history of school" should be underlined. It is an example of hyperbole because it is an exaggeration for effect.

WEEK 6 ⟩ DAY 2

Reading Comprehension:

1. Some synonyms for surly include rude, mean, unkind, dismissive, ungrateful, etc. The behavior of the John Randolph throughout the story should inform the reader's choice. First, he refuses to engage in conversation with the innkeeper; then, he is rude when the innkeeper tries to help him on his journey the next day.

2. Literally, John Randolph appears to be double-checking that he has paid his bill. Figuratively, he is being rude and suggesting to the innkeeper that he should mind his own business since he has already been paid.

3. C - The events of the story reveal that John Randolph is not a great man. He is rude and dismissive to the innkeeper, who he seems to feel he is better than. All the other answers describe the innkeeper's kindness and hospitality, which reflect the truth within the story.

4. C - "There was no signboard to help him" is an example of personification because it treats the sign as if it were a person who was capable of "helping" someone else. The other choices contain only literal language.

5. Answers will vary. Descriptions of John Randolph will likely focus on his rudeness and snobbishness. Descriptions of the Innkeeper will likely focus on his hospitality and intelligence.

English/Grammar Activity:

1. Answers will vary. The answer should contain "like" or "as," since it is supposed to be a simile.

2. Answers will vary. The answer should not contain "like" or "as," since it is supposed to be a metaphor.

3. Answers will vary. The answer should contain extreme exaggeration, since it is supposed to be hyperbole.

4. Answers will vary. The bicycle should be described in a way that makes it seem like it has human traits, since this is supposed to be personification.

5. Answers will vary. The answer should contain "like" or "as," since it is supposed to be a simile.

WEEK 6 ➡ DAY 3

Identifying perpendicular lines, parallel lines, points, lines and rays

1. A   6. C
2. B   7. C
3. A   8. D
4. B   9. C
5. D   10. B

WEEK 6 ➡ DAY 4

Time

1. D
2. C
3. B
4. C
5. A
6. Two hours and twenty minutes
7. 5:15 pm
8. C
9. Twelve past one
10. Three hours and 23 minutes

Unit conversions (minutes, seconds, hours, liters, etc)

1. C
2. 5,700 grams = 5 kilograms 700 grams
3. C
4. A
5. D
6. A
7. 2 days
8. 1 m 64 cm

WEEK 6 ➡ DAY 5

Word problems for unit conversions

1. D
2. B
3. C
4. A

5. C
6. 4 liters
7. 4,500 grams
8. 2 kilograms
9. 9 liters
10. 7:05 pm

Word problems dealing with mass and volume

1. D
2. 24 liters
3. C
4. 1,100 g or 1 kg and 100 g
5. B

WEEK 6 ➡ DAY 6

Answers will vary.

ANSWER SHEET

WEEK 7 🐢 DAY 1

Reading Comprehension:

1. Answers will vary. Students should focus on the king's desire to be flattered and compared to humans, as well as his dislike for criticism.

2. He is attacked, and probably killed, for being honest.

3. C - The actions of the king in Paragraph 6 show that he wants to be flattered. He is "gratified with the lie" and gives presents to the liar. On the other hand, he kills the person who is honest. All the other answers are opinions that could be reasonably disagreed with.

4. A - The idea that the truthful traveler should have lied is an opinion that could be reasonable disagreed with. All the other answer choices are irrefutable facts described by the author within the story.

5. Answers will vary. Students should point out that the story shows that telling the truth can be punished, while telling a lie is often rewarded. That shows that people sometimes just want their opinion validated, rather than seeing the true facts.

English/Grammar Activity:

1. Opinion. "Best team in the whole world" should have been a major hint.

2. Fact. "I know" should have been a major hint, as should the "fever of 101 degrees," which provides evidence.

3. Opinion. The word "mean" should have been a hint. The idea of giving someone a lunch detention for not doing homework seems like an appropriate, reasonable punishment, which does not agree with the idea of the teacher being mean.

4. Fact. Even though the speaker makes a broad claim, it is backed up with several details, such as his number of wins and his impact on the game overall.

5. Opinion. The over-generalization "Everybody loves" should have been a major indicator. "And watch football" should have been another major hint since many people may not watch football.

WEEK 7 🐢 DAY 2

Reading Comprehension:

1. Answers will vary. Students will probably mention that Davenport seems brave and reasonable at a time when others are full of fear and panic.

2. The other people in the statehouse are filled with fear and believe they should just give up and stop working because the world is ending; unlike Davenport, who says they should light the candles and continue working.

3. B - "This is the last great day" is an opinion because we can see that some characters believe it while others (like Abraham Davenport) do not. Since the world did not end, we can infer this was a factually inaccurate opinion.

4. A - Davenport says, "It is my duty to stand at my post as long as I live. So, let us go on with the work that is before us," indicating that he believes the best way to handle the situation is simply to continue with life as usual.

5. Answers will vary. Students will probably point out that most of the fear in the story was born out of the fact that nobody could explain what has happening with the sun and the weather. If there had been a satisfactory scientific explanation at the time, there wouldn't have been any panic. However, in the absence of information, people began to think the worst possible thing: that the world was ending.

English/Grammar Activity:

1. Opinion. Nobody and boring should have been major indicators.

2. Opinion. Most beautiful and I've ever seen should have been major indicators.

3. Fact. Need hydration and can be extremely dangerous should have been major indicators.

4. Fact. The specific timeframe and geographical details should have been major indicators.

5. Opinion. Cooler should have been a major indicator, since what is "cool" is highly subjective.

WEEK 7 DAY 3

Word problems dealing with mass and volume

1. C
2. D
3. A
4. 7 kg 750 g or 7.75 kg
5. A

Temperature (Celcius)°

1. B
2. C
3. 25°
4. 30°
5. B
6. 15°

WEEK 7 DAY 4

Temperature (Celcius)°

1. C
2. A
3. B
4. D
5. C

Rewriting fractions as decimals

1. A
2. B
3. D
4. B
5. C
6. 0.3
7. 0.5
8. 0.5 meter
9. $0.9 = \frac{9}{10}$
10. 0.25 meter

WEEK 7 DAY 5

Various Real World Word related problems

1. D
2. B
3. C
4. A. by 3 minutes
   B. by 1 minute
5. C
6. 1 hour 25 minutes

7. A
8. B
9. A. $319
   B. $278
10. C
11. A
12. D
13. 14°C

WEEK 7 DAY 6

Answers will vary.

ANSWER SHEET

WEEK 8 DAY 1

Reading Comprehension:

1. The mule wants to be an "inside pet" in the way that the lapdog is.

2. The mule has to do a great deal of hard work, while the lapdog just sits around and gets pampered.

3. D - Eat is a verb because it communicates an action.

4. B - The detail that the horse attempted to kick its master coupled with the phrase "perceiving of the danger of their master" shows that the people's primary concern was for the master's physical safety.

5. Answers will vary. If students believe the mule should've been content with its life, they will probably discuss its size and difficulty living indoors in a clean, comfortable manner. If students believe the mule should've been allowed inside with the dog, they might discuss fairness and the mule's desire to live a more pampered life.

English/Grammar Activity:

1. The nouns in the sentence are family (thing), cat (thing), mice (thing), basement (place/thing).

2. The nouns in the sentence are Mr. Pew (person), tow truck (thing), keys (thing), trunk (thing), car (thing).

3. The nouns in the sentence are artist (person), hours (thing), colors (thing), studio (place/thing), painting (thing).

4. The nouns in the sentence are train (thing), tracks (thing), New York (place), Philadelphia (place), ride (thing), passengers (people).

5. The nouns in the sentence are baseball (thing), catcher (person), people (person/thing), stadium (place/thing).

WEEK 8 DAY 2

Reading Comprehension:

1. Based on the opening paragraphs, we know that Gilbert came from an honorable family of brave, heroic people.

2. Answers will vary. Based on the passage, we know Gilbert's mother enjoys the outdoors and likes to read. She seems to indulge Gilbert in his fantasies, but obviously doesn't seem to believe there is a wolf nearby.

3. D - Proud is an adjective (describing word). You can tell "proud" is not a noun because it isn't a person, place, or thing. All the other choices are various people, who are always nouns.

4. D - The text clearly says Gilbert's mother suggested the walk and "felt quite sure that there was no danger." She simply wants to read outdoors and bring her son with her.

5. Answers will vary. Students will probably mention that Gilbert comes from an adventurous family and is eager to become a hero or fight a monster, like a wolf.

English/Grammar Activity:

1. The words that are not nouns are Read and Creepy
2. The words that are not nouns are Into and Framed
3. The words that are not nouns are Happy and Sad
4. The words that are not nouns are Ridiculous and Throw
5. The words that are not nouns are Confusing and Strict

WEEK 8 DAY 3

Various Real World
Word related problems

1. 148°C
2. 4
3. pentagon
4. D
5. $\frac{4}{5}$ of a mile or 0.8 miles
6. C
7. $\frac{4}{8}$ yards or 0.5 yards
8. 4,015 days
9. 482 boxes
10. The outside garbage can weighs more by 67 oz.
11. Theater B seated 308 more people than theater A.
12. Vicky used half a cup of milk.
13. The juice is 450 milliliters.
14. Martha purchased 3 pounds of carrots.
15. Amy eats 50 grams of cereal.

WEEK 8 DAY 4

Various Real World
Word related problems

1. C
2. 13
3. A
4. Right angles, 90°
5. Nina baked 106 pies in total.
6. Pepperoni
7. 101
8. B
9. D
10. Liam bought 36 pens in total.
11. A
12. 4:19 pm

WEEK 8 DAY 5

Placing fractions on a number line

1. $\frac{3}{5}$
2. B
3. B
4. C
5. $\frac{3}{5}$
6. C
7. D
8. $\frac{5}{15}$ and $\frac{11}{15}$
9.

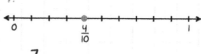

10. $\frac{7}{12}$

WEEK 8 DAY 6

Answers will vary.

ANSWER SHEET

WEEK 9 ⟩ DAY 1

Reading Comprehension:

1. The original deal is that if the doctor cures the old woman's blindness, she will pay him money. However, if he does not cure her, the treatment will be free. This arrangement is described in the first paragraph.

2. The physician lies to the woman (he does not heal her at first), steals from her, and then heals her when it is convenient for him to try and get payment from her, even after he has already robbed her.

3. A - An "agreement" is a thing and therefore a noun. All the other choices are action verbs.

4. D - "I am" is the only use of a to-be verb contained in any of the answer choices.

5. Answers will vary. Students might suggest returning the woman's property, having to do future work for her, having to provide other medical services for free, time in jail, etc.

English/Grammar Activity:

1. The verbs in the sentence are is (to be), trying (action), and catch (action)

2. The verbs in the sentence are rattled (action) and was (to be)

3. The only verb in the sentence is is (to be)

4. The verbs in the sentence are runs (action) and loves (action)

5. The verbs in the sentence are hold (action) and walk (action)

WEEK 9 ⟩ DAY 2

Reading Comprehension:

1. Israel ties a rope around his waist so that his friends can pull him out of the cave as quickly as possible if he runs into the wolf.

2. The first time, Israel wants to confirm the wolf is in the cave. The second time, Israel enters with his gun to shoot the wolf. The third time, Israel goes into the cave to confirm that the wolf is dead.

3. D - "Pulled the rope quickly" contains a verb (pulled), but that verb does not describe Israel's actions. It is the other men who pull on the rope to get Israel out of the cave. All the other choices specifically describe actions taken by Israel.

4. B - The balls of fire describe the wolf's eyes. The text literally says, "He knew that these were the eyes of the wolf."

5. Answers will vary. Students might mention that the other men played an important role by holding the rope and helping Israel get in and out of the cave. On the other hand, some students might argue the other men were cowards for not assuming any of the risk themselves.

ANSWER SHEET

English/Grammar Activity:

1. The words that are not verbs are Toad and Airplane
2. The words that are not verbs are Taco and Screwdriver
3. The words that are not verbs are Artist and Valentine
4. The words that are not verbs are Goldfish and Printer
5. The words that are not verbs are Mouse and September

WEEK 9 DAY 3

Right Angle, Acute Angle, Obtuse Angles

1. C
2. A
3. 1,2,3
4. 2,3,5
5. 1,2,4
6. B
7. C
8. 3
9. 3
10. 2

More rounding problems

1. D
2. 1,300
3. B
4. 160

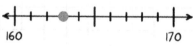

160   170

WEEK 9 DAY 4

More rounding problems

1. 700

600   700

2. A
3. B
4. D
5. to the nearest thousand
6. to the nearest hundred

Patterns and Rules

1. C
2. C
3. C
4. B
5. D
6. Any shape that has 17 circles is fine; One example:

7. 9, **16**, 23, 30, **37**, 44
8. **25**, 43, 61, **79**, ... the fourth number in the pattern is 79
9. Times 4
10. 9, **18**, 36, **72**, 144

WEEK 9 DAY 5

Money

1. Jake. $102 > $67
2. B
3. C
4. D
5. A
6. B
7. C
8. D
9.

Dollars	Cents
1/2	50
1/4	25
3	300

10. $79 and 97¢
11. $4
12. B
13. C

WEEK 9 DAY 6

Answers will vary.

246

ANSWER SHEET

WEEK 10 🦭 DAY 1

Reading Comprehension:

1. The stag is being chased by hounds and is looking for a place to hide until it can escape. This is explained in Paragraphs 1-2.

2. Specific details from the story will vary. The stag is somewhat desperate and hoping others will help it. It is legitimately scared for its life. The stag also attempts to be polite by thanking the oxen. However, the stag is also not a good enough strategist to save itself.

3. B - "Those lazy fellows" is the complete subject because it contains all the relevant information about the subject of the sentence. "Have not even swept the cobwebs away" is the complete predicate because it contains all the actions that those characters have (or have not) performed.

4. D - Saying the master has "a hundred eyes" is an example of figurative language, specifically hyperbole. Other details in the story show that the master is a regular human person, ruling out the possibility that this statement is meant literally.

5. Answers will vary. Students might suggest the stag running immediately after the first check, hiding its antlers more effectively, or finding a different place to hide altogether.

English/Grammar Activity:

1. The subject of the sentence is "Dr. Shapiro." The remainder of the sentence is the predicate.

2. The subject of the sentence is "We." The remainder of the sentence is the predicate.

3. "Almost none of the cars in the race" is the subject of the sentence. The remainder of the sentence is the predicate.

4. "Clyde and Christopher" are the subjects of the sentence. The remainder of the sentence is the predicate.

5. The subject of the sentence is "My dad's truck." The remainder of the sentence is the predicate.

WEEK 10 🦭 DAY 2

Reading Comprehension:

1. Dean Swift shows the delivery man how he should behave by roleplaying and pretending that he is the one delivering something.

2. The dean's servant believes the man has no manner because he just hands over the birds he's delivering without saying anything else. In actuality, he is frustrated that he is not receiving any sort of tip or payment.

3. B - "Mr. Boyle" is the clear subject of the sentence. "Was a sporting neighbor" is the beginning of the predicate because "was" is the sentence's main verb.

4. C - Mr. Boyle brings a duck at the beginning of the story, then a partridge, then a then a quail, and finally a rabbit. There is no mention of a turkey anywhere in the story.

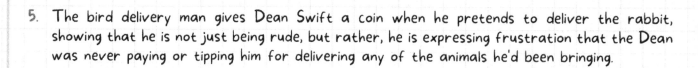

5. The bird delivery man gives Dean Swift a coin when he pretends to deliver the rabbit, showing that he is not just being rude, but rather, he is expressing frustration that the Dean was never paying or tipping him for delivering any of the animals he'd been bringing.

English/Grammar Activity:

1. Incorrect. The line should go after "Ted"
2. Correct.
3. Incorrect. The line should go after "geese"
4. Incorrect. The line should go after "people"
5. Incorrect. The line should go after "young"

WEEK 10 DAY 3

Money

1. $35 and 79 cents
2. $3 and 12¢
3. $29 and 29¢
4. $14 and 66¢
5. 619 dollars and 50 cents
6. $27 and 85¢
7. $45 and 67¢ + 84¢ = $46 and 51¢

Angles

1. B
2. A
3. C
4. obtuse
5. C
6. A
7. C

WEEK 10 DAY 4

Angles

1. B
2. A
3. C
4. A. Acute
   B. Right
   C. Acute
   D. Obtuse
5. Acute
6. 90° Right
   87° Acute
   160° Obtuse
   95° Obtuse
7. It is greater than a right angle.
8. Obtuse
9. It is equal to a right angle.
10. A. 2   B. 3   C. 1
11. C
12. A
13. A. 1   B. 2   C. 2

WEEK 10 DAY 5

1. B
2. C
3. D
4. C
5. C
6. B
7. A
8. B
9. D
10. B
11. D
12. B
13. C
14. A
15. D
16. B
17. A
18. D
19. B
20. A

WEEK 10 DAY 6

Answers will vary.

ANSWER SHEET

WEEK 11 DAY 1

Reading Comprehension:

1. Answers will vary. Students could describe the mice as organized, brave, thoughtful, disciplined, armored, etc.

2. The mice give all their leaders decorative helmets so the other mice will know who to lead and follow in battle, but the big helmets only trap the mice outside their holes where the weasels can start the battle by defeating all the best and most important warriors/leaders.

3. B - "Frequent" is an adjective because it is describing the "defeats" of the mice by providing more detail about how often they occurred.

4. A - The "honor" of wearing the fancy leaders' helmets actually made the mice who had them more likely to be defeated. Even though they were treated as the most important mice, they were also in the most dangerous situation.

5. Answers will vary. Students might suggest measuring the helmets first to make sure they would fit back through the holes or using some other strategy to identify leaders.

English/Grammar Activity:

1. New is an adjective describing car. Purple is an adjective describing paint.

2. Easy is an adjective describing way. Covered is an adjective describing bridge.

3. Scrambled is an adjective describing eggs. Favorite is an adjective describing thing.

4. Younger is an adjective describing sister. Outstanding is an adjective describing student.

5. Quick and brown are both adjectives describing the fox. Lazy is an adjective describing the dog.

WEEK 11 DAY 2

Reading Comprehension:

1. Answers will vary. Students might say Longfellow is thoughtful, high-minded, a perfectionist, slow to start working, a troublesome student, imaginative, etc.

2. Longfellow's teacher tells him to start with a few words and build out from there. That is similar to how adjectives work because they provide additional details and provide extra information. When Longfellow finally picks the turnip, he starts by thinking about what a turnip is like, what it is good for, etc. That's basically like brainstorming a list of adjectives.

3. C - Based on the passage, the reader should be able to tell that a "slate" is something that students used to write on.

4. C - According to the story, Longfellow only wrote about the turnip because it was the thing he saw right in front of him in the garden outside the school when he didn't know what to write about.

5. Answers will vary based on the personal passions, hobbies, and interests of the student.

ANSWER SHEET

English/Grammar Activity:

1. Answers will vary. Uncontrollable, evil, gigantic, menacing, shiny, etc. are all examples of possible correct answers.

2. Answers will vary. Valuable, heart-warming, exciting, fun, boring, special, etc. are all examples of possible correct answers.

3. Answers will vary. Adorable, crazy, out-of-control, annoying, rambunctious, etc. are all examples of possible correct answers.

4. Answers will vary. Old, crummy, stupid, rusty, tired, ancient, cheap, etc. are all examples of possible correct answers.

5. Answers will vary. Favorite, special, customized, personalized, colorful, green, ballpoint, etc. are all examples of possible correct answers.

WEEK II DAY 3

Mixed Math Questions:

1. D
2. B
3. C
4. B
5. C
6. B
7. D
8. C
9. B
10. B
11. D
12. C
13. D
14. A
15. D
16. B
17. D
18. A
19. C

WEEK II DAY 4

Mixed Math Questions:

1. B
2. D
3. D
4. C
5. B
6. C
7. D
8. C
9. C
10. C
11. D
12. B
13. D
14. A
15. D
16. C

WEEK II DAY 5

Large Numbers: Addition and Subtraction Practice

1. C
2. B
3. A
4. A
5. D
6. B
7. A
8. A
9. D
10. D
11. C
12. A
13. C
14. C
15. D
16. D
17. A
18. B
19. A
20. C

WEEK II DAY 6

Answers will vary.

WEEK 12 ● DAY 1

Reading Comprehension:

1. Based on the first paragraph, we know the man provided the animals with food and shelter when things were very cold.

2. The Ox is willing to do work (and even enjoys it) in order to provide for others. The horse and the dog are mostly self-centered and focus on themselves.

3. C - "Chiefly" is an adverb because it is describing/modifying the verb "characterized." Chiefly also ends in -ly, which is common among adverbs.

4. C - Within the passage, it is the Ox who is portrayed as working hard for others. The dog is irritable and only interacts with people it knows will help it meet its needs.

5. Answers will vary. Students should identify that this story is describing the three stages of life: youth, adulthood, and old age. When people are young, they are wild and don't think about the consequences, like a horse. When people are adults, they focus on providing for the people around them, like the Ox. When people are old, they find it hard to put up with things they don't like or people they don't care to deal with, like the dog.

English/Grammar Activity:

1. The only adverb in the sentence is "very," which modifies "old"

2. The only adverb in the sentence is "swiftly," which modifies "flew"

3. "Never" is an adverb modifying "forget." "Always" is an adverb modifying "put."

4. "Extremely" is an adverb modifying "wet." "Freezing" is an adverb modifying "cold."

5. "Rarely" is an adverb modifying "eat." "Usually" is an adverb modifying the "is" that is hidden within "it's (it is)".

WEEK 12 ● DAY 2

Reading Comprehension:

1. Answers will vary. Cimabue is artistic and sees the potential in the young shepherd's artistic ability. Cimabue is also generous because he offers to take Giotto on as an apprentice and teaches him how to become a great artist.

2. According to the text, Bondone allows Giotto to go with Cimabue because (1) he recognizes his great talent as an artist and (2) he believes Giotto is unsuited to do any of the work he knows how to teach him. This is revealed when he says, "I know that the lad can draw pictures wonderfully well... He does not like to do anything else. Perhaps he will do well with you."

3. B - The reader should be able to infer that the charred stick is similar to a pencil because Giotto uses it as a writing/drawing tool during the story.

4. B - In the passage, the phrase "great many" is used to describe how many sheep are in Giotto's flock. "Many" is the adjective describing "sheep," and "great" is an adverb modifying "many."

ANSWER SHEET

5. Answers will vary. Student answers should describe both the scene (a flock of sheep) and the quality of the picture (which we know to be very good, based on the events that follow in the story).

English/Grammar Activity:

1. Definitely is an adverb modifying think.
2. Really is an adverb modifying smart. Responsibly is an adverb describing save.
3. Daily is an adverb modifying rises. Nightly is an adverb modifying sets.
4. Pretty is an adverb modifying scary. Really is an adverb modifying fake.
5. Happily is an adverb modifying laughed. Dramatically is an adverb modifying slipped.

WEEK 12 DAY 3

Mixed Problems

1. C
2. B
3. C
4. B
5. >
6. B
7. B
8. C
9. B
10. A
11. B
12. A
13. C
14. B
15. D

WEEK 12 DAY 4

Mixed Problems

1. A
2. D
3. B
4. C
5. A
6. D
7. D
8. D
9. B
10. A
11. C
12. B
13. C
14. A
15. D
16. C

WEEK 12 DAY 5

Mixed Problems

1. C
2. A
3. C
4. C
5. C

Adding and Subtracting Decimals

1. D
2. D
3. C
4. A
5. D
6. D
7. C
8. B
9. B
10. B
11. D
12. D

WEEK 12 DAY 6

Answers will vary.

ANSWER SHEET

WEEK 1 DAY 7

WEEK 2 DAY 7

1 - E   5 - B
2 - D   6 - H
3 - A   7 - G
4 - C   8 - F

WEEK 3 DAY 7

Tape with a letter **D**

WEEK 4 DAY 7

WEEK 5 DAY 7

WEEK 7 DAY 7

WEEK 6 DAY 7

1 - A
2 - C
3 - D
4 - E
5 - B

ANSWER SHEET

WEEK 8   DAY 7

1 - Bathrobe
2 - Soap
3 - Towel
4 - Shampoo
5 - Hairdryer
6- Comb
7 - Toothbrush
8 - Mirror

Key word - **BATHROOM**

WEEK 9   DAY 7

A - 4
B - 5
C - 2
E - 1
D - 3

WEEK 10   DAY 7

A - 9
B - 14
C - 1
D - 12
E - 5

WEEK 11   DAY 6

Bug 4
Bug 5
Bug 8

Made in the USA
Middletown, DE
19 March 2020